Reading the Way of Things

Towards a New Technology of Making Sense

Reading the Way of Things

Towards a New Technology of Making Sense

Daniel Coffeen

Winchester, UK
Washington, USA

First published by Zero Books, 2016
Zero Books is an imprint of John Hunt Publishing Ltd., Laurel House, Station Approach,
Alresford, Hants, SO24 9JH, UK
office1@jhpbooks.net
www.johnhuntpublishing.com
www.zero-books.net

For distributor details and how to order please visit the 'Ordering' section on our website.

Text copyright: Daniel Coffeen 2015

ISBN: 978 1 78535 414 4
Library of Congress Control Number: 2015960677

A CIP catalogue record for this book is available from the British Library.

Design: Stuart Davies

Printed and bound by CPI Group (UK) Ltd, Croydon, CR0 4YY, UK

We operate a distinctive and ethical publishing philosophy in all
areas of our business, from our global network of authors to
production and worldwide distribution.

CONTENTS

Preface

This book was many years in the making and has taken many forms before becoming this. It stems from the ideas that motivated my dissertation, written for my degree from the UC Berkeley Rhetoric Department, in 1997–1998. The title of that admittedly more academic tome is *Read This Text*, an attempt to suggest that rhetoric is the logic of reading and engaging difference.

But the motivation really came from the incredible experience I had teaching the introductory lecture for the Rhetoric major at Berkeley — and the experience that followed with having those lectures podcast by the university. Suddenly, I was in conversations with a breadth of people from all over the world — an astronomer in Kansas, a high-school student in Georgia, a philosophy student in Turkey, a marketing executive in Mexico, a writer named Doug Lain in Portland.

This experience was augmented by the education I received after my doctorate, working with the artist and filmmaker Marc Lafia, who taught me new ways of making sense of the visual, the network, and the computational. His perhaps unknowing mentorship opened my eyes, wide.

And all of my thinking owes a considerable debt to the poet and sophist, Lohren Green. Together, through long and elaborate conversations, we turned grad school into an experience of living thought. And then his incredible books — *Poetical Dictionary* and *Atmospherics* — inspired, prodded, and provoked me in the best possible sense. My thanks to him are boundless.

I dedicate this book, then, to these teachers and those students who have made my thinking all the more delightful.

Reading, I enter a relational contract with whatever *material, accepting its fluency and swerve. I happen to be the one reading.*

— Lisa Robertson

1

Introduction: The Technology of Sense

To consume media today is to consume an endless parade of declarations, insistent beliefs, claims to knowledge and truth, debates that go nowhere. We see it, of course, in the political realm where the same cast of characters repeats the same phrases, claiming the same old positions, as if choosing from some shared multiple-choice list. We see it in medicine and food, in history and science: *Raw food is the healthiest! Cooked food is the healthiest! Kale is a superfood! Don't eat too much kale!* We see it in how people talk about movies: *A silly spectacle! The story was not believable! Thumbs up! Thumbs down!* And, in our private conversations and even private thoughts, we agree or disagree, repeating the same canned lines: *Gay marriage is a right! I have to eat more blueberries! That movie was stupid but fun!* Through it all, we carry on as if these are the things that can be said about the world, as if this is the set of possible claims and it's our job to choose one or another.

Meanwhile, the way in which these opinions and claims are reached, shared, and processed is never questioned. Rarely do we hear something that operates on totally different terms. Even more rarely do we consider rejecting the terms themselves and inventing our own. We simply assume that that's how people talk about food, talk about movies and books, talk about politics. But, as Marshall McLuhan argues, we are always enacting an invisible environment of technologies — from electricity and the internet to the alphabet and the novel — that we don't notice but which is, in fact, a historical construction that distributes bodies, power, sense, knowledge, emotion, as well as the very construction of ourselves. We could say these technologic environments are ideological, which they are, but in a wide sense

1

of ideology that entails the ways we make sense of the world, what we consider of value, what we consider true, how we stand in the world towards others and ourselves.

We are always operating with certain tools and technologies that dictate the possible outcomes of what we can say and think. Just look at what the computer did to how we work and interact with each other; then what the internet did; now what mobile computing is doing to the social as well as the private, how time, language, and relationships are redistributed. The very manner in which we conduct ourselves, construct ourselves, changes as the tools we use change. McLuhan argues that the alphabet is one such technology that privileges sight over sound and linearity over what he calls *allatonceness* (sight comes from *there*, he argues, while sound comes from all around us, all at once). Each letter in the alphabet has its place; together, they make a word; words go together in a row to make a sentence; and so on. It's a factory, an industrial enabler.

Many of these tools and technologies that surround and define us are not as slick or obvious as the iPhone or as readily recognized as the alphabet. And what makes things even trickier is that these tools and technologies vanish into the background as what we consider true, what we take for granted as the way of things. So bringing them up is difficult as it's hard to see one's own way of seeing. And it makes the person who brings them up — I suppose that's me — seem potentially insane.

I want to argue that the very manner in which we form, share, and digest information is a symptom of a technology of language. That is, we assume language to be a certain thing — a system of referents that signify meaning — and then go on with our lives using this technology. So when we, for instance, watch a movie, we look for the signs and symbols that map back to a meaning — *a meaning that already exists*. This meaning may be something learned in school, such as the Oedipal complex or patriarchy or capitalism. Or it may be something so close it never occurs to us that it is something we've learned — ourselves. In both cases, the architecture of making sense — the mechanics of reading — enacts the architecture and mechanics of a certain model of language that suggests meaning *already exists*, is stable, and it's our job to manipulate marks and signs to point to it.

Our use of a technology of reference that points backwards and elsewhere —to something bigger, broader, and more abstract such as concepts, ideas, and categories — inhibits the creation of the new, inhibits the possibility of creative, critical thinking. After all, if we're using a tool that is predicated on what already exists, how can we think something new? If we're using a tool that demands we look beyond what is right here to what is bigger, broader, and more meaningful, how can we take what is right in front of us on its own terms? This is at once a matter of creativity and ethics, of how we stand towards time and each other.

In this little book, I want to propose a different technology of sense-making — a technology of things, concepts, operations, principles, and mechanisms working together — that doesn't rely on our present conception of language. This entails considering everything from how we consider a thing to what we consider knowledge, truth, and how we access it — what a word is, what an image is, how the social operates, what our place in it is. I want to suggest that if we shift how we make sense of things, we in turn shift our very relationship to the world, to each other, and to ourselves. From this perspective, nothing is more politically fraught than the manner in which we make sense of the world, than the technology we use to engage and process: than how we read the way of the world.

I am calling this technology a form of reading — what I'm calling *immanent reading*. I want to extend the definition of literacy to include more than the deciphering of letters-as-code; to define literacy as a critical, creative act of making sense. Immanent reading, I propose, is a technology that fosters a

3

radical democratization of reading, a technology that enables and empowers anyone, reading anything, to make fresh sense of it without relying on traditional sources of knowledge and expertise. With new sense-making, I like to imagine the world might become more beautiful, more interesting, more vital.

The Making of Sense, or Exemplary Reading

You look at a painting. It's one of the "great" paintings, so we're told: Picasso's *Les Demoiselles d'Avignon*. How do you make sense of it? How do you enjoy it? And how do you think you're *supposed* to make sense of it? What do you think you need to know before you're allowed to enjoy, understand, and comment upon this so-called masterpiece? Is there some kind of knowledge you need to have before you're allowed to make your way through it? Or can you just begin anywhere at any time and think, feel, and say what you want? Is there a proper time for looking, some kind of origin point that marks the path towards understanding this enigmatic work of art?

The way we read things — books, films, art — and the ways we're taught to read things tells us a lot about how we construct the availability of knowledge. What do we even count as knowledge, as making sense of something? And who is granted access to this sense-making and under what conditions?

The way read things and the ways we're taught to read things tell us as well about how we construct access to delight, to pleasure, to the full array of affects and sensations that come from books, films, and art. Are these feelings different than knowledge? Who is granted access to the spectrum of sensations that literature, cinema, and art offer?

And who has the right to speak of these things, of this knowledge and these feelings?

Now, I am not asking about the so-called canon and access to what we tend to call the "great books" and "masterpieces." I am talking about something at once much simpler and more complex: the very act of taking up the world in front of us —

from *Ulysses* and Picasso to John Cassavetes, a chair, and TV's *The Office*. When we engage anything, we come to that thing with certain assumptions about how to make sense of it, what right we have to consume it, enjoy it, know it. I will suggest there is continuity in how we engage — or "read" — things that runs from Joyce's *Ulysses* and Picasso's *Les Demoiselles d'Avignon* to *The Office*, the glass you drink from, and the chair you're sitting on right now. But let's focus for now on things like books, films, and art before we get to everyday things that have a way of eluding our attention precisely because they're so familiar.

A few good teachers aside, we are taught from grade school through grad school that in order to make sense of these things, we need the tools, language, and understanding of something else — usually, something equally if not more esoteric. Let's return to *Les Demoiselles d'Avignon*. We want to understand it. But what does "understand" mean? The flurry of facts about the painting — the name of the artist, the date it was made (was it made on one day?), the art movement (who decides what's a movement and what's not? who decides what's in a movement and what's not?), the materials? To understand, do I need to know the biography of the painter? If so, which biography? What makes up a biography? Is there such a thing as a basic fact? Or are there always acts of weaving that stitch these facts together into a text(ure), an argument that makes meaning (whatever that is) of them?

Anyway, we're standing in front of this Picasso painting which is a tad odd and we want to understand it. And what is our first instinct? *To turn away from the painting!* We lean down and read the writing on the wall, no doubt written by an expert well-learned not just in the history of art but in the history of this painting and its elaborate pedigree — things we, as laypeople, know nothing or little of. This, to me, is a telling symptom of our technologic environment of language: to make sense of something, we turn away from it and seek something else. It's almost childlike, running to the parent to explain the weird, scary shadows on the wall.

When we actually read what's on the wall, we tend to get all kinds of information and some esoteric words. We learn some basic facts — born here, died there, painted there, also painted some other things. And we probably read about Picasso's relationship to women and, maybe, we read about how this painting confronts the male gaze in an act of either defiance or contrition, depending on who wrote it. In any case, to understand the painting we believe we have to look elsewhere, to turn away. The sense of this painting, we believe, isn't there in front of us but in our knowledge of other things — history, gender, the history of presentations of the female body, the biography of the painter, a brief overview of the times (again, according to whom?).

These might or might not all be good things to know. But are they necessary to know in order for me, standing directly in front of the painting, to make sense of that painting? The persistence of the writing on the wall, and the ubiquity of headset museum tours, tells us that looking at the painting does not suffice. If I want to appreciate it — understand it, make sense of it, even enjoy it — I have to turn away, not just to learn the facts but to read the experience of someone else who knows better or more than I do: an expert. This expert is the keeper of sense, the key to unlocking or decoding what's sitting directly in front of me.

The same goes for books. When we read Joyce's *Ulysses*, we believe we need to know about Joyce and his life; Dublin at the time; modernism as a movement; Homer, no doubt; the contemporary construction of gender and race; the history of literature; the way of consciousness — ego, superego, id, Oedipus, and such. If we're adventurous, we might read some feminist or gender theory from Cixous or Judith Butler; probably some Marxist theory; certainly some Freud and Lacan; some Derrida could help; other modernist literature such as Virginia Woolf;

maybe other books by Joyce. In all cases, we're not reading the book in our hands. We're reading something else as a way to make sense of this book right here and now. This book, this painting, is not just what it is or how it treats us. This thing right here is an example of something else, something bigger and more important — ideas, concepts, theories, historical circumstances — things we imagine to be broader as somehow "grounding." (But does meaning need a ground? Is meaning a tree, the roots grounding the branches and leaves of texts? Or, as Deleuze and Guattari suggest, is it a rhizome, sprouting here and there as opportunity yawns, with no center or ground holding it all together?)

I call this mode of making sense — this turning away and seeking explanation from something bigger, this arborescent mechanics — *exemplary reading*. In exemplary reading, we make sense of things as an instantiation of something else. This something can be a category such as a genre (*The Maltese Falcon* is classic noir), an idea (*Blue Velvet* is all about the Oedipal complex), ideology (*Gone Girl* is patriarchal), history (Cubism was radical for its time), biography (Picasso had troubled relations with the women in his life). In all cases, we make sense of what we're experiencing through things that have come before and have stood the test of time. This painting, this book, is just a moment of that bigger thing.

Here's a straightforward and common example of an exemplary reading: "The books of William Burroughs are postmodern." The thing (in this case, the vast and varied writing of Burroughs) is determined by an idea (the postmodern) that we imagine precedes Burroughs' books and, in some way, makes them possible. "Postmodernity" — whatever that is — is big and broad. It stands outside the everyday as part of the fabric of sense itself. When we read Burroughs' admittedly odd books, we discover their sense in and through the bigger, more secure sense of the postmodern. To continue Deleuze and Guattari's figure, "postmodern" is the fixed roots and Burroughs' writing is the branches or perhaps leaves.

Now, this mode of reading-by-example can take varied forms. For instance, we can suggest that Burroughs is not an obedient example as we argue how his books are *not* postmodern — they're part of the mystical tradition. Or we take up another example of postmodernity — Thomas Pynchon — and we talk about how Burroughs' paranoia differs from Pynchon's in that Burroughs is not paranoid at all: to him, the world is at war hence one had better keep a good lookout. We end our reading, then, with a new understanding of the category "postmodern." In this strategy, a particular thing is in a relationship with a category either as an instantiation, a rebel, or a modifier: Burroughs is postmodern; Burroughs is *not* postmodern; Burroughs shifts the terms of postmodernity. In all instances, we don't as much read Burroughs as we confirm the category or idea of "postmodern."

Another mode of such exemplary reading, and one that remains popular in universities, is *ideology critique*. We read something in light of a predefined "cultural" or "ideological" category such as gender, race, sexuality, Marxism, psychoanalysis. We then say how Burroughs challenges the dominant mode of heterosexuality or its vision of homosexuality or we pinpoint his misogyny or we invoke his revolutionary, anti-capitalist stance. In all of these cases, we are reading Burroughs as an example or counter-example — as *evidence* — of a given category, a category that itself is not part of the reading but is being confirmed or disconfirmed. The category stands outside both Burroughs' text and our reading like a firm ruler capable of measuring anything, even Burroughs' careening prose. Ideology critique is a common assignment in college classes, as Freudian readings of *Vertigo*, feminist critiques of *Deep Throat*, and Marxist analyses of *The Wire* abound.

These kinds of reading can be powerful, useful, illuminating, even revolutionary as hegemonic categories such as patriarchy and capitalism come crumbling down — or at least are shaken. This is how we take on those big ideas that dictate how we think and feel and act. Thinking of the world as categories and their children, if you will, is a common and effective way of making sense of this world. It's how we teach toddlers to see the world: *Put all the blue blocks here, the red ones there.* Things, we are taught, are instances of ideas, concepts, and categories that are not themselves up for grabs. Blue is blue; boys are boys; big is big.

But there are other ways of making sense, other ways of construing the relationship between this thing here and ideas, concepts, categories, biographies, and histories. Exemplary reading, as a way of making sense, is not without its ideology and historical heritage. It assumes there are certain things that are not up for grabs, that are not to be made sense of, along with the books, paintings, and art. Exemplary reading rests on the assumption of assumption, that there are certain things we can just count on. Why? Because experts have told us.

There is something disrespectful about such a mode of making sense. Rather than make sense of *Les Demoiselles d'Avignon* on its own terms — whatever those are — we make sense of it on Freud's terms, as inevitably told to us by an expert. We assume that our own faculties, our minds and imaginations and capacities to feel, are not enough. And, frankly, often they aren't. Most of us are filled with idiocy we never question. But one such thing we never question is why that sans-serif writing on the museum wall has a right to intervene in my experience of looking at this nutty painting! Sure, it knows some things. But I bring all kinds of knowledge and experience to that painting and that painting brings all kinds of sensations and affects that don't need to be mediated by some art historian. If I hone my skills, my attention, I can make beautiful sense of that Picasso painting without having ever heard of Picasso or patriarchy or Oedipus or Cubism.

Why do we do this? Why do we reach for something else, something we imagine as bigger and more prestigious, more controlling — an expert, genre, ideology, history — to make sense of this thing we have right here in front of us? What's wrong with us, or with the art, that we feel we need something else to understand it — and even enjoy it?

Well, I imagine there are all kinds of reasons. For one, many of these things are complex. They disturb the world we know. Upon first impression, and maybe even third and fifth impressions, *Les Demoiselles d'Avignon* doesn't look like paintings or women we know. *Where are these women?]* (Avignon is not enough of an answer.) *Why do their bodies bend like that? Is that one wearing a mask? What's going on here?* So, like children who seek answers from established authorities, we ask art historians: *What does this mean? What can I enjoy here?* And then we might ask our therapist: *Is it ok to feel pleasure or disgust here? What does that mean?*

But even this answer begs for more exploration. Children do ask questions when they don't understand and yet, even before the question is asked, they have already made some kind of sense of it. How could they not? Whatever they see, they see and that seeing nudges them this way and that, makes them think of other things they've seen, perhaps only in their dreams. In any case, they may be asking but that event of question-and-answer is not the movement from ignorance to knowing but a testing of how a private and idiosyncratic sense fits into an established sense. The child's question, then, doesn't seek merely to know per se but to know how what she thinks fits into what adults think.

Sense happens, no matter what. You look at that Picasso painting, you read Joyce's *Ulysses*, and something happens. The question is what value do you give to that sense? How do you make sense of that sense? It's a lot more comforting to quote some writing on a wall than to launch into your no-doubt-strange, mostly inchoate experience.

This exemplary reading is constitutive of a social architecture. How we make sense of things (what philosophers call epistemology) and who makes sense of things (the social order) are intimately intertwined. Exemplary reading cascades down from a point, like a pyramid. On the bottom, everyone has to look up at the top, the Big Idea, to make sense of their lives. And who's right below that point? The expert.

This is a multi-millennial struggle between the priests and the flock. Do we need the priests to give us access to God? Or, as Jesus suggests rather adamantly in words, deeds, and his very being, is the Word made flesh? Is it always already in all things — and hence no priest is required? Can we access the truth of the world, whatever that could and does and might mean, on our own? Or do we need a special class of privileged folks to dish out meaning as they deem fit?

I am not suggesting some elaborate plot by curators, professors, and academics to keep us under foot. The social and personal architectures of knowing are complex, always being built from multiple sources all interconnected — desire, ideology, power, history, circumstance, need. The reality is that life is complex and can be scary. It can be very reassuring to put something as crazy and unsettling as *Les Demoiselles d'Avignon*, Burroughs' careening prose, Joyce's prodigious and allusive *Ulysses*, John Cassavetes' *Faces*, or Chris Marker's *La Jetée* in a proper, snug place. We engage these things and experience exceedingly odd sensations, a kind of delirium or befuddlement. We feel strange or stupid. So we lean on others, on experts and facts and inherited interpretations so we don't have to wrangle the idiosyncrasies of our own private experiences. Ideology doesn't come from above; it streams from all of us in all directions.

This same structure, or a variation of it, runs through how we make sense of all kinds of things, everyday things, not just the so-called great works of literature, film, and art. For instance, often when we read books, watch TV or movies, or just people-watch, we *identify* with the subject. We imagine ourselves as them — and then we pass judgment.

Think about the Martin Scorsese film, *Goodfellas*. We are literally walk into and through the life of the mafia in the 1970s via Ray Liotta's character, Henry Hill. All around him, crazy, violent, exotic things happen — people have strange nicknames, feet are shot, there are menacing exchanges. But, as viewers, we are made to feel more-or-less safe thanks to our identification with a character who's not all that bad. Sure, we see Henry beat someone up, but someone who sexually assaulted his girlfriend — so, well, that's ok with us. Other than that, we can go along with him.

This is often how we make sense of art and people. Someone walks into a bar wearing pleated khakis or a nose ring or skinny jeans and we think: in order to wear that, they'd have to be this kind of person because that's the only way I could ever wear any of those things. We don't assume they have their own elaborate, distinctive way of making sense of the world. We move to a category — what type of person does such a thing? — and put ourselves in their place. Of course we do, because we all exist under the same category of being human in this time and place.

But let's imagine, for a moment, another way of making sense of the world. Rather than classifying and *identifying*, we *confront*. Let's consider John Cassavetes' *Faces*, a difficult movie, especially considering today's standards of narrative. Watching *Faces*, or any Cassavetes film for that matter, we are not allowed to identify with anyone. Every character is equally within and out of reach. They laugh, cry, scream, mumble, but never invite us in. Our experience is never one of identification, either with a character or a category. Rather, we are confronted just as we confront: the film goes as it goes, I go as I go, and what happens in between is what happens. It's a stew of effects and affects and associations.

Sure, I can read the Criterion Collection's liner notes. I can read Wikipedia. I can dismiss the film as boring or arty or as just not something I like. But none of those things help us, finally, make sense of this film — this film that refuses a foothold, that won't let us like or dislike anyone, that won't let us rest on realistic or unrealistic, that refuses genres such as noir, art-house, indie (if those even are genres!).

When we watch TV, we often seek to see ourselves. *You're a Rachel*, we'll tell someone after watching *Friends*, but *I'm a Monica*. That is, we seek ourselves. Rather than trying to explain Picasso through Freud, we try to make sense of *Friends* through the enormous shadow of ourselves — as if ourselves were one clear category. Ask people about a popular book or film and they'll say, *I like this character but don't think it was realistic that he did this or that.* The criterion of judgment is some notion of ourselves and what counts as real. But how then are we to grow? If we always bring things back to a certain notion of ourselves, how are we to become, to be different, to expand ourselves?

All of which is to say, the way we make sense of things is rarely to engage the things. We don't confront the things before us as something *different*; we confront them as something we already know, as if everything fits into pre-ordained buckets of knowledge, as if those buckets weren't themselves created, as if buckets and categories themselves weren't buckets or categories that might impede knowing. Exemplary reading, whether seeking basis in biography, ideology, theory, history, or ourselves, avoids the difference and newness and downright oddity of the things we experience. To make sense, we look backwards to the already known rather than looking to what's in front of us and wondering: What new world flourishes here?

This is the case not just for seemingly special things like books, films, and art but for everyday things. We sit on chairs as we're supposed to sit on chairs; drink from glasses we assume are made for that beverage. We assume houses have living rooms and bedrooms; that romance involves two people of the same or different genders; that work demands 50 hours a week of our lives, at least. In these cases, we are blinded not by concepts and categories but by habit and familiarity.

What happens when those things we experience every day suddenly pop from the dim din of habit? What happens when the things we take for granted come to life, assert themselves, show different sides? And, for our purposes here, what happens when we *seek out* those other sides, seek out other ways of making sense of the same old things. What happens when rather than taking things for granted, we actively see anew, actively see difference, see differently? What happens when we look for the strange in the world?

Take the martini glass. From one angle, it's just a glass, albeit an outdated symbol of urban sophistication. But let's consider the martini glass, not based on symbols, history, or any particular knowledge. Let's just consider the experience of the martini glass. It's odd, for sure. Most glasses and cups make carrying and drinking the contents easier — they have handles and high edges. Not the martini glass. It's wide with a thin grip. It is, in fact, difficult to drink from. But what makes it particularly odd is that it is used to serve a drink that makes drinking from any vessel more difficult. A martini is a strong, strong drink. With every sip, your capacity diminishes. And yet you're bridled with this unwieldy glass! It's as if the glass itself is challenging you: drink this hard drink, which makes drinking from this glass increasingly more difficult. Can you handle it? Can you keep cool enough? Suddenly, this everyday thing becomes an elaborate tool of training, teaching you to become cool: intoxicated yet steady, passionate but with an unwavering hand. It's not just a symbol of cool; it's not just an arbitrary form. The martini glass is a pedagogy in the way of cool.

The way we make sense of things is not neutral or natural. It is part and parcel of a certain construction of sense. And these ways we make sense are constructed in such a way that we don't think about them at all: it's just what we do. This doing might seem obvious, once pointed out, when it comes to esoteric texts such as the great books, artworks, and films — whatever those are! But this mode of reading, in which we make sense of the thing in front of us through other sources, is sense-making as a way of domesticating the wildness of things. All those private, odd sensations from watching *Faces*? I shoo them away and "understand" Cassavates as a *neo-realist* (or some such serious-sounding category).

In this book, I'm trying to suggest that there are other ways of making sense, ways that are beautiful, astounding, exhilarating, life-affirming, that maintain and even celebrate the wildness of life! I am suggesting that there is a different architecture of sense-making that recasts the entire dynamic between you, thing, knowledge, experience, pleasure, and world. Rather than turning away from things and seeking concepts and rather than wallowing in our habit and selves and our quest for sameness, we can confront things on their terms and engage with their difference. This is a different way of making sense, what I call *immanent reading*: reading a text — whatever that text may be — on terms immanent to it and the very act of reading it.

3

Making New Sense, or Immanent Reading

What is "immanence"? Well, immanence is tricky. It is what pertains to a thing, what is *of* a thing, what is *of* the experience of a thing. But I want to be clear that I am not suggesting that a text — I will use the word "text" interchangeably with the word "thing" — has an essential or reducible meaning. The immanence to which I refer is not *in* the text. It's not inherent as a secret or a soul: it is revealed in how this thing unfolds *in* and *with* and *as* the world.

So why call it "immanent"? Because I want to look at a mode of reading, a mode of making sense, that does not begin with an external term — a genre, theory, concept, or yourself — but takes up the world from *within* the world, as part of the world, rather than from outside the world (wherever that is). That is to say, I do not want to assume I know what postmodern literature is and then read Burroughs and wonder how he fits. Rather, I want to begin with Burroughs — his strange rhythms, his even stranger figures — and see where it takes me. I don't want to *know* the text; I want to *go with* the text. The category of postmodernity, as well as the category of literature, may or may not be taken up by the immanent reader but in any case this is not the starting point. Following Gilles Deleuze, we might call this mode of reading *empirical* in that it tends to what is there, both visibly (words, images) and invisibly (affects, ideas).

One might be tempted to say exemplary reading is deductive, beginning with the general term, and deducing the specific term: Burroughs' writing, as the particular, is an example of the general term, postmodern literature. And immanent reading is inductive, beginning with empirical evidence — Burroughs is paranoid, Burroughs is meta — and ending in a concept such as postmodernity.

But immanent reading is neither deductive nor inductive. It doesn't travel up and down between concept and experience, one substantiating the other. The entire relationship between particular and general, along with the concept of example, is reoriented, turned from a vertical axis to every-which-way axes. Immanent reading begins with the thing at hand — Picasso's painting, Burroughs' writing — and follows where it might go, depending on who's doing the looking. It might take you to a concept. But it might not. And even if it takes you to a concept, it doesn't want or seek to end in said concept; any concept is just one point along a meandering path determined by the exchange between this and that, between thing and reader.

But this is not to say that a text, or the reader or even the event of reading, is solipsistic, sealed into itself. A thing is a multiplicity, *a way* of taking in other things in the world and making sense of them, processing them, assembling them just so. To read immanently is to follow — and perhaps construct — a network of elements, concepts, affects, possibilities, notions that hang together in just such a way for this text.

Immanent reading begins with the text — the text that is made of other texts, inevitably — and lets it guide. Or, perhaps, it begins with the readers' encounter with the text and goes from there. This means the reader does not look for a key or an answer to explain it; there is no secret waiting behind or hidden within the thing. This means no concept, no theory, no genre, no historical circumstances rear up and demand compliance. A thing goes as it goes. The immanent reader follows this way of going.

Which means no peeking behind the text to find an author or an intention. The immanent reader doesn't look to the biography of the author for clues to the meaning of the text. There is no moment that can be mapped back to the life and times of the writer, as if the life determines the words (and not the other way around! Burroughs' work demanded his nutty life, not the other way around — or perhaps the other way around, as well). To an immanent reader, there is no privileged access to a thing, whether that thing is a book, a painting, a film, a building, a martini glass, or a job. A painter may say she meant to portray the anguish of contemporary life but that doesn't put an end to the process of reading. The creator of a work is another possible reader who does not hold any authority over the sense of a text.

To grant the author authority over his words is *not* to read the text. After all, why read *Lolita* if we can just ask Nabokov what it means? But as any reader of *Lolita* knows, the power of that book does not reside in its meaning but in the very *experience* of reading it, the way the language — the prowess of the prose, the rhythm of the words — plays across the palate and belly and throat and loins.

Or consider this. You're talking with your spouse. You say you're going out tonight, *again*. He sighs, turns away, and says, "*Fine.*" You ask: "Are you sure you're fine?" Again, he sighs, looks away and says, "*Yes.*" Do you take him at his word? Has he provided the truth of what he claimed? Is he really "fine"? Of course not. Words are *experiences* that not even the speaker or writer of them owns. Once uttered, the words are in play, equally for everyone. We are all readers, even of ourselves.

This may seem counter-intuitive. After all, the writer writes the words, the painter paints the painting, so they must know what it means. But look at it this way. A writer uses words to write but he doesn't *own* those words. A writer doesn't invent new words; that's not what makes a writer. And even when he does, his language is still subject to the laws of language, even when he pushes the syntax and the grammar. If the author were to invent his own words and his own grammar, no one could read his writing at all. It would be gibberish. No, words belong to all of us and none of us. When a writer writes, he borrows and steals words — words that are as much ours as they are his. (The same can be said of images and the visual: it's all there for all of us; the art lies in the *how*, not the *what*.)

This is not to say that the biography of a painter or the words of a writer are not interesting, that they don't serve any function in a reading. The facts that Burroughs shot and killed his wife may inflect your reading of Burroughs but it in no way *determines*, once and for all, every reading of Burroughs. Rather, it is to say that these facts and an author's words about his own text do not have any more *authority* than we do as readers. There is no privileged access to a text. There are as many ways into a text as there are readers, and more. In *The Death of the Author*, Roland Barthes argues that the author is a relatively recent historical invention: "The author is a modern figure, a product of our society [...] emerging from the Middle Ages" (142).

Once we remove the author — not the one who writes but the one who has *author*ity over his writing — the very notion of a text and what it is to read that text changes dramatically:

> Once the Author is removed, the claim to decipher a text becomes quite futile. To give a text an Author is to impose a limit on that text, to furnish it with a final signified, to close the writing. Such a conception suits criticism very well, the latter then allotting itself the important task of discovering the Author (or its hypostases: society, history, psyche, liberty) beneath the work: when the Author has been found, the text is 'explained'—victory to the critic. Hence there is no surprise in the fact that, historically, the reign of the Author has also been that of the Critic, nor again in the fact that criticism (be it new) is today undermined, along with the Author (147).

With no author, with no guiding theory, a text has no answer. It becomes an open thing, a multiple thing, with no kernel, no center, nothing hidden that needs to be revealed. To the immanent reader, there is nothing outside the fray, nothing stable that can ground a text — not an author, genre, theory, or concept.

The immanent reader does not *penetrate*; she *follows*. She does not look for an *answer* or *meaning*; she proliferates *possibilities* of going.

In a world of immanent sense-making, the world is not a hierarchy that begins with categories and concepts and then cascades down. Everything — and I mean *everything* — is in the mix, sloshing about, intermingling (or not). This is not a matter of deductive versus inductive analysis; this is a fundamentally different architecture along with a different conception of architecture. Here, structures are in motion and concepts, categories, and ideas are part of the mix, not outside it. There is no clear up or down, no fixed ground or orientation. It's like reading in outer space. Or, rather, it *is* reading in outer space.

Immanent reading does not entail *deciphering* a text. Immanent reading operates with a non-symbolic model of language. Rain does not always mean moral instability; red can be more than blood; family dynamics are not always Oedipal. To the immanent reader, signs don't point elsewhere. Signs are *motivated*: they are a life unto themselves (cloying, for instance, doesn't just point to a meaning — it is itself cloying. Or a martini glass that is not just a sign of cool but *demands* cool). Symbols, like ideology and authorship, are pre-determined by something beside themselves — a reality or concept or idea that exists elsewhere. The immanent reader does not come to the thing already knowing what it is, for then she wouldn't be reading. This reader is *generous*, permitting the text its want.

In fact, I want to argue that the very architecture of exemplary reading — this particular leading to that generality — comes from a referential conception of language. That is, we imagine words are examples of something more general, namely meaning. This then dictates how we read in that we look for meaning from the signs and symbols that a text offers.

But immanent sense-making begins with a different conception of language, one in which words don't just *refer* to things but are *networked* with things in complex and ever-different ways. A word is not a *sign* but a *gesture*, a creative act that distributes sense. A word is an action, not a record or mark of meaning (or at least it's always *also* an action). I want to say that there is no language per se, as if language were something separate from us that could be studied, as if language were a system with set rules and behaviors. What we have in the place of language is rhetoric, tropes, performative events that construe the world and distribute bodies. The example Deleuze and Guattari use is the utterance "Guilty" as said by a jury or judge. Suddenly, the body of the accused is moved physically, socially, and discursively. This model of how words work gives us a different concept of things and a different mode of reading them.

"[C]ontrary to deeply rooted belief," Deleuze and Guattari write in *A Thousand Plateaus*, "the book is not an image of the world. It forms a rhizome with the world, there is an aparallel evolution of the book and the world; the book assures the deterritorialization of the world, but the world effects a reterritorialization of the book, which in turn deterritorializes itself in the world (if it is capable, if it can)" (11). This is to say, a book is not a reflection of the world; it doesn't as much write *about* the world as it writes the world itself. It takes up little pieces — gestures, affects, words, images — and rearranges them just so. A text doesn't comment upon the world; a text creates a different world.

A text — a book, a concept, the nape of a lover, an apple, a glass of whiskey or whiskey in general — *reveals* itself in its very mode of existence. (Unless its revelation is a masking. The films of David Lynch, for instance, turn on secrets never revealed to the audience. Think of *Blue Velvet*: why has Isabella Rosellini's husband been kidnapped? Who are those people? There's no mention of riches or ransoms. Or *Twin Peaks*: Kyle MacLachlan's dream ends with Laura Palmer whispering in his ear. Or *Lost Highway*, whose characters refuse to divulge the extraordinary things they've seen. The finale, as if to parody this secrecy, finds

Robert Blake whispering in the ear of Bill Pullman, too low for us to hear, revealing *that there will be no revelation* — not even to the filmmaker.) No need to peek over a text's head to see what's going on behind it. It's all right *there* (which is why it's empirical).

To read immanently is to turn with a thing, a body, a text. It is to follow the path forged by this or that. Reading is not digging or sifting. You can't wipe away the words to get at the meaning. Meaning and word are so intimately wound up with each other as to be inseparable (although they're not the same). Maurice Merleau-Ponty says they are intertwined, that the visible and invisible components of a word form a chiasm. I like to think of them as marbled, the sensuality and the concept running through each other, flowing in and around each other. In any case, you have to read the words and everything they entail — meaning and sensation and ambiguity. You have to reckon what's *there*.

Now, as Barthes claims, immanent reading tends not to be very popular at universities. Why? Because it belies the very structure of the university by undermining the privilege of the so-called expert. To perform an exemplary reading, one must presumably be an expert in the field at hand. If I want to say that Burroughs is or isn't postmodern, then I must be an expert in postmodern literature. And professors *must* be experts; such is the basis of their claims to power. But an immanent reader is an *amateur* through and through. He doesn't bring expert, exhaustive, or sanctioned knowledge to his reading. He brings himself and his skills.

"The amateur," Marshall McLuhan writes, "can afford to lose" (93). That is, the amateur does not need to defend his position or sanction a field of knowledge. The amateur is free to spin the world, to say anything, to bring into play any elements. What does the amateur have to lose? As Shunryo Suzuki-Roshi says, "In the beginner's mind there are many possibilities, but in the expert's there are few." The amateur sees possibilities where the expert shuts them down.

Immanent reading empowers the person standing in front of a Damien Hirst, watching a David Lynch film, reading James Joyce to make sense in his or her own way. The immanent reading is radically democratic. The reader no longer needs any special information or any field of expertise; she doesn't have to read the writing on the wall next to the decaying shark carcass.

But just because an amateur is not bound to a field of knowledge doesn't mean that reading is easy. On the contrary, it demands attention, skill, *thinking*, an active metabolism. To be empirical means to heed what's there, what's happening now. You can't just lean on a concept or category; you have to be alert.

Reading and making sense involve a certain distribution of bodies. At the very least, there's the body reading, the body read, and existing knowledge. The different technologies of reading architect these relationships differently, casting different postures of the reader, different ways of standing towards the body read and towards existing knowledge.

Exemplary reading casts the reader and existing knowledge outside the teeming fray of time and its transient bodies. As an exemplary reader, I stand here, unmoving, able to see the flux of other bodies. Without implicating myself in their flurry, I can reach in, grab something, and place it within the steady, firm structure of knowledge that stands behind me (or above me): *James Joyce's* Ulysses *belongs here, thank you very much.* In the mechanics of this architecture, the reader does not move; knowledge does not move. And the act of reading puts a stop to the movement of things; in this case, *Ulysses*.

Immanent reading involves a different architecture and mechanics. The reader is moving along with all the things. And so is all that knowledge! Everything is moving — at different speeds, sure, but it's all moving. A banana, for instance, moves faster than a rock. But it's all moving. The reader, in this case, has no sure footing to reach in and grab something. And there's no edifice to place it in, no bucket or category, as this is a mostly liquid world (there are solid and gaseous states as well as other strange hybrid consistencies such as viscosity).

The exemplary reader is not only sure-footed. She assumes sure footing is what making sense demands. She *grounds* her arguments and tries to build the absolute and definitive one.

The immanent reader, meanwhile, doesn't have sure footing. But because she never had sure footing, she doesn't see it as a problem. In fact, it never even occurs to her that she should have ground beneath her. So when she reads the world, makes sense of things, she doesn't seek to ground it. It doesn't occur to her that her reading could be definitive. She just wants it to be interesting, beautiful, vital. She makes sense of a world in motion while in motion herself — her body is changing, the world around her is changing, and hence her sense-making is always changing. Just because she finds rice to be her wonder food now doesn't mean rice is a wonder food always for everyone. It's a wonder food here and now for her.

Exemplary reading and immanent reading: these are different architectures of the reading event, different postures of how one stands in and towards and with the world. The exemplary is the domain of the sure-footed expert who stands between things, the uninformed, and sanctified knowledge. The expert emerges from the culture of the priest and his church where there is first the word of god, then the priest who grasps it and who, in turn, brings it to the flock. The way to knowledge — to god — is through the expert-priest. The architecture is a hierarchical pyramid that moves towards a singular point while cascading down to the mob. Particularities are subsumed by generalities. And only the master, well-heeled in his learned ways, can decipher the vicissitudes of particularity and give them a proper home — this book belongs in this genre, this one doesn't.

To an immanent reader, a text is what Deleuze and Guattari call a rhizome. There are multiple ways into a text, multiple ways of making one's way through it, and the whole thing — text, reader, world — is moving. There is no front door. Nor is there a back door. And the text won't stay still long enough for the reader to exhaust it once and for all. Pick your point, wherever it may arise, and see what happens. There is no privileged access and an immanent reading is never definitive (even if thoroughly persuasive). This is the jurisdiction of the amateur who is not tethered to a discipline or knowledge community but is free to follow the text wherever it goes — and even to places it doesn't.

The Terms of Exemplary Reading vs. Immanent Reading

- Signs that refer vs. Gestures and events that create and distribute
- Reader as agent of knowledge vs. Reader as agent of events
- Allopoietic vs. Autopoietic
- Will to the definitive vs. Will to the multiple
- Reader as expert vs. Reader as amateur
- Pyramidal/hierarchical vs. Rhizomic/networked
- Linguistics vs. Rhetoric
- Geometry (three dimensions) vs. Calculus (four dimensions)

Immanent reading is radically democratic. It eliminates the need for a learned expert, empowering the individual standing in front of a Jeff Koons to make sense of it. Of course, someone else's reading may be better than his — more interesting, more intriguing, more provocative, more engaging. And our individual may defer to that other reading. Or, he may say, "That Dr. Coffeen, while interesting, is full of it! Jeff Koons' basketballs are not beautiful in that there tank. They are frustrated, like fish out of water, that they cannot dribble or be dribbled. These floating basketballs are not 'decontextualized,' as Coffeen says. They're lonely and frustrated."

Isn't this the power, the threat, of bottom-up media? The rise of the web and its network structure undoes the very pyramidal architecture of the expert. Many decry the nonsense spouted by the masses and long for a certified word from above. But, in the network, a reader must decide which reading works best for her. It's no longer a matter of going to the library and citing some source with the appropriate letters after his name. There is no recourse to the expert to close discussion. All there is is the reading. And then another reading. And then another. It's readings all the way down.

In any case, this immanent reader does not need the master's word to reckon her experience. She needs skills, not knowledge. She needs attention, engagement — *participation*, not *expertise*. Immanent reading is an open invitation.

4

The Way of Things: Multiplicity, Affect, Style

If we're no longer to always see things as referring elsewhere, as gaining their meaning from something else — even their utility — we need to understand the way of things.

A thing is one thing that is many things, "a complex nexus, an assemblage" (D&G, TP 3). A thing — a text — is a multiplicity, an assemblage of elements visible and invisible. The visible elements are obvious — a book has words, maybe some images, a font; a film has sound and images; a painting has colors, shapes, perhaps some forms; a flower has scent, color, size, density; a glass of tequila a taste, color, weight. But all these things have invisible traits, as well. Of course, sound and smell are invisible but they are obviously sensual and measurable. When I say invisible I mean the moods and affects of a thing. Sometimes, especially with complex texts, the visible and invisible elements have strange and shifting relations.

We might want to say that an affective state is always subjective, that the text gives us a sensual experience but the affective experience is solely subjective and not part of the thing — *the movie* is violent but *I* feel horrified. But I think with a little consideration, we can see that this is not the case. First of all, and perhaps most obviously, when I experience something while watching a film — fear, delight, joy, exuberance — whence this state? Is it only from my absolutely personal well of memories, thoughts, and experiences? Or could it be that *the film* affected me? Well, of course the film affected me. But then perhaps the question is: did the film affect me and others the same way? Yes and no. Clearly, we are all different and hence enjoy different experiences of things. This is made all too obvious when you're in a theater and you're the only one not laughing. But even at these moments, you can understand *why* those around you are laughing. You may not experience the mirth but you can see the mirth *in the film*.

This is to say, things are affective and these affective states and my affective state may very well be different. This is a difficult distinction to maintain but it is important. It is difficult because while we feel we can objectively measure the visible states of a thing — its size, color, density, smell, sound — we can't objectively measure a thing's invisible states. There are no tools, no numbers we can ascribe, upon which we can all agree. Visible states are quantitative; invisible states are qualitative. And only quantity is objective, we believe, while qualities are always subjective.

And yet I maintain that things, texts, have affective qualities — "have" is not quite the right word; these affective states are constitutive of a thing — that are not the same as my affective states. I can say that the films of David Lynch are creepy and funny; that the art of Joan Miró is whimsical and joyous; that my son is shiny, grounded, and exuberant. And when I say these things, I am not saying that *I* feel this way. I am saying that these things *are* this way.

In *The Critique of Judgment*, Immanuel Kant discusses precisely this strange phenomenon in which someone claims that what seems to be a subjective taste is, in fact, objective. Now, Kant was a rationalist through and through and was therefore skeptical of the senses. What we experience sensually, he maintained, cannot be trusted. Only what is conceptual and hence universal can be trusted, known, objective. He therefore argues that what happens when we make objective claims about subjective taste is that we are making a claim about the possibility of our mental faculties being moved in such a way. That is, a claim about a work of art is not properly speaking objective yet nor is it subjective. The art operates at neither the level of conceptual understanding nor purely subjective whimsy: it operates on the mental faculties (reason, imagination) but in a non-conceptual way. What is universal about aesthetic experience, to Kant, is the possibility of a similar effect on these faculties across people.

This is an exceedingly odd and convoluted reasoning (and one I enjoy precisely for these reasons). Immanent reading has no need of such elaborate convolutions because immanence is not rational. This technology of reading is *phenomenological*. Kant, as a rationalist, does not allow affect a voice in the mix so that even when discussing a work of art, Kant appeals to non-affective descriptors — the beautiful and the sublime — and to the mental faculties but not to affect. For Kant, our perception of a thing moves from the sensual to the conceptual; mood, affective states of being, are not an essential part of experience. But from a phenomenological perspective, a thing is at once physical, conceptual, and affective. No one term determines the others; it's all one big mish-mash. Here, concept is not king. Rather, the visible and invisible worlds, in the words of Maurice Merleau-Ponty, are intertwined. A thing is a network of diverse strands, run through with notions, moods, ideas, concepts, memories. Even the most banal of objects — say, a nail clipper — bears the memory of its making and its use, concepts of grooming, the history of technology, the possibility of a menacing future.

Consider a human body as a text. It has so many complex functions not all of which can be reduced to totally physical behavior. I am blood and liver and hair and skin and desire and anxiety and love and dreams and eyeball and nose and kidney. And I keep changing — physically and affectively — as time passes, as food passes, as I interact with the world. I am teacher, writer, son, father, friend — and each of these is multiple, each of these shifts as circumstances shift. I am this thing that is many things and that keeps changing, always and necessarily. I am, like all texts, "a machinic assemblage of bodies, of actions and passions, an intermingling of bodies reacting to one another" (D&G, TP 88).

A book, a painting, a flower, a film, a meal: each is a more-or-less complex amalgamation of elements working more-or-less in tandem. Perhaps the colors or words or tastes fuse into a greater whole; perhaps the different words, colors, tastes ricochet off each other or ignore each other or forge distinct experiences. Tequila can often enjoy a distributed flavor palette, carrying itself along distinctive taste channels on the tongue — vanilla, citrus, pepper, grass, leather, sun. Bourbon, meanwhile, tends to be unified, falling across the tongue in a consistent ooze. But, with the tequila, the differences do not unite; nor do they contradict. The different strands form a complex harmony, at time disjunctive, parallel, indifferent, synergistic.

But if a text is multiple, what makes it *a* text? Well, this all depends on the circumstance. As a thing is writ with multiple elements, it is writ with multiple internal limits. So a reader could read one particular element within a thing, making that element the thing read. For example, my body is made up of my toes, nose, eyes, blood, liver, heart, desire, loves, needs, wants, dreams, fingers, lips, tongue, taste. But I may only read one of these things, say, my big toe. In this case, my big toe is the text which is itself made of multiple things — a nail, skin, wrinkles, hairs, cuticles, *shmutz*. The limits of this or that thing is configured by the reading event: who is doing the reading, where, when, why, how. A foot fetishist and a doctor would make very different sense of this big toe.

This, among other things, lies at the heart of certain debates about medicine: What are the terms of a body and its dis-ease? Some claim a holistic approach, that everything from blood to memory to desire affects the health and vitality of a body. Others suggest that medicine is basically all physical: let me look at your blood under a microscope, even if I never meet you, and I can tell you what's wrong. Different doctors operate with different limits, internal and external, of a human body. They distribute the body and its relations to the world, including disease, differently. See Georges Canguilhem's *The Normal and the Pathological*.

These limits may extend wide and far and remain nebulous. A martini glass is part of a network that includes whiskey glasses, shot glasses, pint glasses, neon signage, the *Thin Man* movies (but that's from my perspective because I've seen *The Thin Man* and have been drunk from whiskey glasses; my son may also enjoy martini glasses but his reading, were I to ask him, would inevitably follow a different path and construct a different network of elements). The multiplicity of a thing extends beyond its immediate physical boundaries; a thing contains its history and its culture. Jacques Derrida finds traces of other texts every time he reads, one text bleeding, echoing, quoting, ricocheting against other texts, what he calls intertextuality. The oeuvre of William Burroughs, for example, might include his "novels," his essays, his interviews, his readings of his novels, his shotgun paintings, his cut-up poems, his collaborations with Brion Gysin and Kerouac, his letters to everyone, most notably to Ginsberg. It might also include his diaries, pictures of him, all the writers and texts he references — Denton Welch, Jean Genet, Norman Mailer, Carlos Castaneda — and those he doesn't reference but that certainly run through his writing — Rabelais, Philip K. Dick, even Nietzsche. Then again, perhaps I want to limit myself to his so-called novels (I qualify because I'm not sure what a novel is and whether the term applies to Burroughs' books) or only his mentions of alien homosexuality or his rhythm. Frankly, I'm not sure it matters. An immanent reading has no desire, no goal, to be definitive or final. An immanent reading is one moment, one possibility, of how a text can go.

A text is an assemblage of signs and effects, of gestures and affects, of moods, modes, and meanderings, of forms and functions. It is not just many things — many things that manage to cohere without unifying — but the very manner of taking up those things. It is an *assembling*, not just an assemblage. A thing enjoys an internal process of differentiation that we might call its metabolism, its way of processing the world. Such is its way, a way that affords the reader multiple paths, diverse sites of entry or pick-up, numerous possibilities for taking, cutting, stealing, borrowing, following.

Human bodies are presumably made up of the same stuff — blood, skin, organs, limbs, muscle, cells. But look around you and see all the different ways these same elements hang together: this one slouches, this one jaunts, that one twitches. A thing is not just the sum of its parts. A thing is the mode of putting all the parts together. A thing is not just visible and invisible stuff. It is temporal, as well, a four-dimensional text. A thing doesn't just go; it goes this way. It goes with *style*.

Style is tricky to grasp. Here's how Paul Ricoeur puts it: "A style is the promotion of a particular standpoint in a work which, by its singularity, illustrates and exalts the eventful nature of discourse; but this event is not to be sought elsewhere than in the very form of the work" (Ricoeur 137). Deleuze tells us that a style "is not a signifying structure, nor a reflected organization, nor a spontaneous inspiration, nor an orchestration, nor a little piece of music. It is an assemblage, an assemblage of enunciation" (Deleuze and Parnet 4). It is not a concept or idea that sits outside of a thing as style. It is that which forges, manipulates, and assembles bodies of all sorts, including concepts and ideas. Style is not determinative, at least not prior to the event or expression. It is not a law that legislates from afar, taxation without representation. Style is a function, what Merleau-Ponty calls "a manner of formation." Style is the fourth dimension of a body, not just its temporality but its rhythm, the shape of its time in the world.

Style is not an essence. It does not exist prior to the thing. Nor does it reside deep inside, pushing the buttons, driving the ship. Nor is it the means one adopts, say, to liven up an otherwise boring performance. Style shows itself, or rather, forges its very existence, in the process of production, emerging at the point of contact between and amongst bodies.

Style is not just a heeding of the world. It is *this* manner of heeding the world. Style is what *this* body does with the world, *how* this body does with the world. Style is metabolic, a singular body's manner of consuming and distributing the world and, in the process, of creating itself: a productive consumption. It is the rate and mode of consumption and distribution, the manner and speed with which a thing takes up the world and puts it to work. One way of speaking about style is to say that it is the way in which one *appropriates* the world — takes it in and spits it back out.

Once again, look around you. See the different ways different bodies hold themselves, the different speeds and postures with which they tend, and attend, to everything around them — other people, information, light, hair, eyes, scent, air. Every thing consumes the world in its own way and, in so doing, creates itself. This is what we call *comportment,* the way a thing hangs in the world, the way it carries itself in the world. Comportment is at once a mode of interaction with the other things — an appetite as well as a touch — and the manner in which a thing holds its different elements together. A swimmer, a linebacker, a German Shepherd, a Chihuahua, a toddler, an adolescent, an elderly woman: each carries itself differently, assembles itself differently, emphasizes certain things and not others, leans more-or-less forward, more-or-less quickly, more-or-less upright, more-or-less attentive to different things. Each thing is more than a set of traits. Each thing is a way of going.

Style is not something done *to* the world but *with* the world (*as* the world). Our very perception of the world is already a particular configuring of that world; it is a giving-shape to the many elements that present themselves to the perceiver. You and I are walking down the street. I notice some things, you others. And we do very different things with those perceptions. There is no moment we can possibly experience that is free of our styles.

Even so-called inanimate objects enjoy a style. Put any two drinking glasses together and you'll quickly see two modes of making sense of beverage, container, and consumption. And these different styles, these different glasses, interact with other styles. Drink tequila in a whisky glass and you'll lose the delicate nose of the agave; drink whisky in a tequila glass — tall and thin — and the whisky will fail to open. This world calls for the right style for the right thing on the right occasion.

A thing — a text — is a multiplicity of elements, physical and affective, hanging together by the emergent and particular function of style.

Example 1. Ways of Taking Up the World: Stealing and Poaching in the Wachowskis' Bound and The Matrix

With *Bound* and *The Matrix*, the Wachowskis proffer two modes of reckoning cinema, and perhaps all art and maybe even all identity: stealing and poaching.

The Matrix is a product of unabashed thievery, a pastiche of visual history, copping innumerable tropes from everything from the spaghetti western to video games. The Wachowskis take whatever they need to invent their universe, chewing up inherited images with abandon. This mastication is not interpretation. *The Matrix* is not a take on the video game *Street Fighter*; it doesn't interpret *The Good, the Bad, and the Ugly*; we don't view the work of Sergio Leone differently after seeing the movie. This is not homage to Katheryn Bigelow's *Point Break*, even if she taught us that Keanu can run and the camera can follow, closely. No, *The Matrix* is not homage; it is not a deferential or humble film. It is an entirely new beast born from multiple and disparate parents — a bastard hybrid, if you will. And a virile one: this mule can foal (Burroughs, WL 34).

This is filmmaking as all-consuming appetite: *I'll take that and that and that, thanks very much.* Images are ripped and riffed, a shameless thievery. This is mixing at the limit, the strategy of MixMaster Mike and Christian Marclay, turning the found into sound, forging one's own territory from the fodder of others. Thievery is beyond the pale of reference just as it is beyond the reach of *différance*; this intertextuality does not undermine the thief. On the contrary, the thief makes the things of the world so much his own that the terms of propriety shift; the deed is passed as a new world is forged. This is a consumption so thorough that while we can perhaps see traces of former identities we can by no means say that these images belong to anyone else, that they belong anywhere else than right there.

This is in fact the very plot of the movie. *The Matrix* is not, as it may seem, about questioning the line between lived and virtual reality. On the contrary, the film secures the line that separates dream from reality, the virtual from the real. We believe Morpheus; we believe that there is a difference between the real and the virtual and we want to make this distinction firm again. It is not until the second film in the series that we are introduced to radical doubt as Morpheus shifts from truth-teller to fanatic, Neo's powers work against (or is it with?) the machines, and even the Oracle herself becomes a questionable source. In the second film, we are sure of nothing.

But in the first film, we witness a story of theft just as we watch a theft in motion (that is to say, the film itself). The machines steal the electricity of the humans; the humans steal the machines' "souls" as they render machines useful, always serving human ends. Competing thieves, then, each trying to steal the other, to consume the other, to turn the other's mode into one's own. Isn't this precisely what the Wachowskis do — take the production of others and put it shamelessly, gleefully, to the production of themselves? Is film machine or human? Perhaps, the Wachowskis tell us, film is the very place where man and machine meet so as to mutually and productively steal from each other: a symbiotic theft forging a new being, a cine-being.

If *The Matrix* is an exercise in thievery, *Bound*, the Wachowskis' first feature film, is an exercise in poaching. Unlike *The Matrix*, *Bound* is an unabashed genre film, a rendering of noir. Here, rather than stealing images, the Wachowskis enter the image economy of an existing genre, making do from within an existing space. For Michel de Certeau, to poach is to create one's territory within the territory of another not by stealing but by operating, by doing, by moving. Hence, the Wachowskis situate the film at the precise juncture of the economy's conduits, the passages along which the images circulate.

As the film poaches on noir's familiar images — desire, greed, crime, the underworld — the camera follows the diverse paths of their circulation: down pipes, through Doppler's rippling effect on toilet water, through walls inflected with prejudice and assumption, carried along vibration, obscured by habit. The plot turns on the ability or inability to read these signs so as to make something happen — to get rich, to survive, to love. Caesar, the mobster, is utterly oblivious to his girlfriend's lesbianism (until it is too late); after all, she's so feminine. Hence the ex-con "tomboy" lesbian, Corky, also mis-reads Violet, the moll. After all, she's so feminine.

But Violet, like the film itself, is a poacher, inhabiting the skin of the mobster moll in order to make her own way. She even whores, a sign that, to Corky, confirms Violet's heterosexuality. But as de Certeau claims, poaching is the strategy of those without property, of the conquered, those stripped of their own place. Poachers appear to be acting in a familiar way; they exhibit all the "right" signs, like the worker who sits at his computer, ever-dutiful, all the while writing his novel. Poachers make use of the signs of others but in their own way, to their own ends, for their own pleasure. Violet sleeps with men as a way of making money in order to one day slip away and forge her own space. In the meantime, she operates on the territory of the known, exhibiting all the right signs even as she creates her own world from within the world of others. But it is a world that only exists in the going, in the decisions; Violet cannot make a world that is strictly speaking her own. So she makes her way through the territory of others, poaching on their signs as she pleasures herself.

Bound, like Violet, poaches on the territory of the known, on the familiar signs of noir. The film crawls into noir and kicks around with a certain perverse delight, engaging the known signs only to send them astray (but not too far; take a sign too far astray from its home and you become a thief), extending noir's images according to its own sapphic appetite. This is quite different from *The Matrix* which consumes images with another kind of delight, the delight of making the world one's own, of no longer having to tread on someone else's territory: the delight of stealing.

5

Things Happen

This thing that is many things moves. It wiggles. It prances, it speaks, it stinks. It frolics, agitates, provokes, enlightens, annoys, beguiles, seduces. It whines and moans. A text *does* things, all sorts of things.

A text *performs*, directly and indirectly. When we speak, even when we write, we intone. We inflect. There are no words uttered without intonation, without inflection, without style. The very act of saying something is part of the meaning we express, whether we like it or not. We can't separate the *what* from the *how*. Sarcasm, humor, flirtation: these all turn explicitly on *the way* things are said. When we speak and write, our words do not neutrally declare our intentions and desires. Our words are inflected by our palate, drenched in our resonance. The same phrase said by ten different people will be ten different experiences, perform ten different events.

We take this for granted as we make our way through the world. A child says everything's fine but you know it's not. How? Well, his tone, his mode, his look. We do not take people at their word; we take them at their action, an action that *includes* their words but is not *determined* by their words.

All things perform, not just words. Ten different martini glasses yield ten different drinking experiences. Of course, in this case, the differences may be so slight as to be uninteresting. So take ten different chairs, ten different apartments, ten different nail-clippers: the experiences will vary from one to the next, sometimes quite significantly. Take ten different books, ten different paintings, ten different films and the difference expands exponentially. This is all to say, there is no pure sitting or dwelling or nail-clipping and certainly not reading. Each of these entails a what (a thing) and a how (a style). Things are not just *in* the world; they *perform* actions on, to, and with the world.

The immanent reader is attentive to all these elements, including the relationship between them. An immanent reader does not just read for *what* a text says but for *how* it says it — as well as the relationship between the what and the how. Much happens in this space — irony, humor, seduction, hypocrisy. Ignore this space and you miss the world happening.

Take the Platonic dialogues. One may believe everything Socrates says. From the series of pronouncements Socrates makes, we can assemble a system and call it "Platonism." The immanent reader, however, finds it difficult to take Socrates at his word. After all, Socrates engages in dialogues; there's no reliable or stable narrator telling us what's going on. Plato's dialogues are plays that have characters, settings, and plot. And in these dialogues, Socrates does all kinds of things — he makes jokes, he contradicts himself, he fondles his interlocutors, he gets drunk. He renounces lust while ogling a young man; he declares love to be the ultimate calling while he himself is in a lustful frenzy; he gives an impeccable speech denouncing speech-writing. In the Platonic dialogues in general and in Socrates in particular, the reader doesn't find Platonism. He finds a way of life, gestures of living. He finds irony.

We do not communicate via concepts and codes alone. We communicate via actions and affect. When we speak and write, we do not convey meaning devoid of body, action, and affect. Our words do things, all sorts of things. This is what the philosopher J.L. Austin calls the performative: words that in their very saying *do* things. His examples include a wedding vow, a bet, the christening of a boat: "I do," "I bet you," and "I name you" do not *describe* the actions, they *perform* the respective actions of getting married, making a bet, naming a ship. These are explicit performatives. But all words do things (the title of Austin's book is *How To Do Things With Words*). Words move us.

They persuade, bore, enlighten, titillate, enrage, inform.

Deleuze and Guattari inflect Austin's performative. They use the word "order-words":

> [W]e call *order-words*, not a particular category of explicit statements (for example, in the imperative), but the relation of every word or every statement to implicit presuppositions, in other words, to speech acts that are, and can only be, accomplished in the statement. Order-words do not concern commands only, but every act that is linked to statements by a 'social obligation.' Every statement displays this link, directly or indirectly (TP 79).

And, for Deleuze and Guattari, this is what language is: the set of all order-words at any given time (85). Language doesn't refer; language assembles, arranges and rearranges, territorializes and deterritorializes.

The question an immanent reader asks is this: What happens in the very saying, writing, marking, filming?

A text is in motion. Its meaning is not something that *is* but something that *happens*. Any text — book, film, flower, food, laugh — literally takes us up just as we take it up. Our senses are distributed by it as we are nudged this way and that. I love watching my son watch a movie, his facial expressions shifting relentlessly, the movie steering him this way and that. A book does this explicitly, literally choreographing the movements of our body. We read it left to right, one page after another. Now add the invisible movements, or what I've called the *affective* movements, the way a book moves your emotional state, your moods. Things act on us just as we act upon them.

A thing moves. But how can this be? How can a text, especially a written text or a painting, be in motion? Well, every time a text affects the world, this effect is necessarily different. You and I don't just make different sense of Burroughs; we make a different Burroughs — just as Burroughs makes a different me and different you. Every reading is different. And in every reading, the thing is remade, more-or-less. I want to say that a text *is* all of its possible effects. And hence it is something — *this* set of effects — and yet still open, still happening, necessarily. A text is a becoming, a stipulated, bound becoming.

But even on its own, in the absence of readers, it is an operating metabolism, a process of taking in the world and making sense of it. Every thing enjoys different speeds and flows, affective and conceptual trajectories that go this way and that. Things are, in many ways, alive.

This happening of a text is limited, bound by its own comportment, by what it is and how it goes. Which is to say, *a text has an infinite number of possible shapes, as many shapes as there are readers and more. But the text remains bound by its own constitution, by its particular play of elements.* A text is a bound infinity.

A text is a Calder mobile: it has an infinite number of permutations depending on the environment, the nudge of the wind, the inertia of a spectator's gaze. And yet this or that mobile is bound by *its* distribution of weight and balance; its shape is not determined per se by the environment. It cannot spin any way whatsoever. But it can spin any number of ways within the limits of its comportment. (Consider comportment again. Stop and look at the people sitting or walking around you. Each person has his or her own style, her own way of putting a body together and propelling it through space. This comportment is a calculus of spine, weight, sentiment, memory, gait, speed, rhythm. Each of these people can be distended — within limits. They remain bound by what they are, by how they go.)

Consider the distance between one and two, and the distance between one and a million. We can say the distance in each is infinite. But is it the same infinity? Is infinity a generality? Or are there different shapes — or shapings — of infinity? We call such accounting for such variations in infinity "calculus." A differential equation has a limit that is nonetheless infinite or perhaps infinitely approached. Consider the Non-Terminating Non-Repeating Decimal, the NTNRD. Pi, for example, is a NTNRD. It's infinite but extended to infinity in a manner absolutely particular to it. And the fact that it is not just infinite but infinite *in this way* matters. The trajectory of a missile, among other things, depends on such differences.

Like an equation in differential calculus, a text is a bound infinity, at once infinite and limited. This equation is what I am calling the way of the thing.

When we eliminate the fixed boundaries of a thing we do not eliminate all boundaries, all limits. On the contrary, we proliferate them as limits are constantly, relentlessly emerging, internally and externally. A thing goes as it goes. It is a shape in motion interacting with other shapes in motion. Its limit is not an external term that binds it but is an immanent term that pervades it. (One way to read the different tactics of Derrida and Deleuze is via their respective conceptions of the limit. For Derrida, the limit is ambivalent, seeking to bind but always failing, always bleeding. For Deleuze, a limit is productive, multiple, and infinite. It is the very manner, the style, with which this or that takes up the world, the way this or that goes. Derrida reads texts from their limits, beginning at the point at which a limit bleeds, undoes itself. Deleuze picks up a book from its middle, following its intensities. Derrida is slippery. Everywhere he looks, he finds slipping and sliding. To read for this slip and slide is to deconstruct a text. Deleuze doesn't slip and slide — he folds, multiplies, follows. To read Deleuze is to enter an alien world, a world always already in session. Look at how their writings, their readings, begin. Derrida begins with a question about a question. Deleuze begins mid-stride, a conversation that has always already begun. Here are the first sentences of their respective books on Nietzsche — Derrida's will always and never have begun; Deleuze's is already in session, moving quickly. Derrida:

"The title of this lecture was to have been *the question of style*."
Deleuze: "Nietzsche's most general project is the introduction of
the concepts of sense and value into philosophy.") A limit does
not stand guard over a thing but *is* the very way a thing goes. The
limit moves, shifts, changes, a shape in motion. A thing *is* its
limit. Or, rather, a thing *becomes* its limit.

Limits are not to be overcome; they are to be lived through.

Example 2. The Moving Image: Deleuze, McLuhan, Klée, and More

"In short," Deleuze writes, "cinema does not give us an image to which movement is added, it immediately gives us a movement-image" (C2). That is to say, the film camera does not capture stills to which movement is later added by the projector, by an external media; that would be to miss movement all together. "Movement," Deleuze tells us via Bergson, "is distinct from the space covered." Movement is more-or-less continuous while the space covered is divisible. Hence, "you cannot reconstitute movement with positions in spaces or instants in time: that is, with immobile sections."

It is not that cinema invents the movement-image; Bergson discovered the concept independently. But is cinema the only art to proffer the movement-image? Prior to cinema, or outside of cinema, are there examples of the movement-image? In what sense, if any, can we say that an ostensibly still image *moves*? Is this movement the same as a movement-image?

In *The Medium is the Massage*, Marshall McLuhan claims that "[v]isual space is uniform, continuous, and connected" (45). But that doesn't seem right to me at all. Look at a painting by Matthew Ritchie. I suppose in some sense we can say the space is continuous and connected. But uniform? And what counts as continuity? Ritchie's work may not move in any linear fashion but it most certainly undulates: there is a distributing (and not just a distribution) of intensities, of speeds, of temperatures. The eye does not take in the work all at once; consumption is not immediate. *But nor is the painting:* this will not have been a matter of the viewer making the work move. Rather, the viewer moves *with* the painting, with its flows and lines, its vertical and horizontal axes, with its speed of vibration.

We cannot say, then, that the movement of the work is the movement of the viewer, of his mind or even of his eyes (although it is both of those things as well). The *painting* takes the viewer on a journey, not to an imaginative place, not to concepts or ideas (at least not necessarily; there may very well be a conceptual speed and intensity as well, not to mention a speed of communication between and amongst concepts), but a perceptive journey. As Deleuze and Guattari maintain in *What is Philosophy?* a percept is distinct from perception, from a perceiving subject. The movement at work in Matthew Ritchie's painting is the movement of the image.

In his reading of the French artist Gérard Fromanger, Deleuze maps the distribution of temperature in Fromanger's photographs/paintings. "[I]n each painting," Deleuze writes, "there is a voyage, a circulation of tones." The image, then, is not still, not uniform or continuous. Indeed, "[a] circuit of exchange and communication begins to be established in the painting." That is, colors speak across the canvas to each other, lines criss-cross, they swerve and bend. There are points of inflection, moments at which things turn: yes, *moments*.

I can't help but think of the so-called abstract paintings of Modernism. Pollock, like the roving camera of film, put himself in motion, writhing over the canvas. Miró became obsessed with birds, with the possibility of a line that could take flight, unobstructed. Paul Klée's line, like Miró's, wiggles and prances and folds and bends; at times, there are arrows so we can keep track of all the movement. There's a great Klée drawing I saw recently. It was not as rounded as I imagine Klée's usual work; there was an odd geometry as the lines turned at sharp angles, forming a strange portrait. The title was, "Moderately Slow." We call Calder's work "mobile." (The mobiles are 3D Mirós: it is not that movement is made explicit; it's that movement shifts from two to three dimensions.)

This circulation of intensities, this communication of tones, these lines of flight: is this the movement-image of Deleuze and Bergson? How does this movement of the image relate to the moving image of cinema? What makes the cinematic image different from the painting or photograph? From Bazin to Deleuze, there seems to be agreement that movement is the distinguishing factor. But if we agree that images do move, what distinguishes the movement of cinema from the movement of a Klée drawing?

According to Deleuze, the movement-image of cinema involves the perpetual modulation of matter: "the movement-image is the object: the thing itself caught in movement as continuous function. The movement-image is the modulation of the object itself" (C2 27). The movement-image is not a representation, a capture, but "matter itself" (33). But this can certainly be said of a painting or photograph as well. As Merleau-Ponty argues, Cézanne's apples are not representations of apples at all: they are apples, again and anew (SNS 12–15). Great images do not refer, they do not point: they are matter, they are the world modulating itself before our very eyes.

Deleuze therefore seems to locate the point of distinction elsewhere. "Photography," he writes, "is a kind of 'moulding': the mould organises the internal forces of the thing in such a way that they reach a state of equilibrium at a certain instant (immobile section). However, modulation does not stop when equilibrium is reached, and constantly modifies the mould, constitutes a variable, continuous, temporal mould" (C1 24). The movement-image is "a transformation of the mould at each moment of the operation" (C2 27).

This is deceptively complex so let me follow its different threads. Deleuze claims that the internal forces "reach a state of equilibrium" and then suggests that this is an "immobile section." But is an equilibrium necessarily immobile? Kant claims that confronted with beauty, say a flower, the faculties of the viewer are set in a motion that will not resolve; he calls this "free play" (62). And yet, unlike the sublimity of a storm, beauty affords a kind of harmony of the faculties: an equilibrium of sorts is reached and yet free play persists.

Of course, for Kant, this free play is a free play of the faculties; it refers to the motion of a mental state, not of the object. But if we assume the phenomenological perspective, the seer and the seen are intertwined: the motion of the mental state is continuous with the motion of the object. It may not be a matter of a pure reflection, of an unadulterated echo, but it is a matter of a repetition, a continuous bloc of becoming that includes object and viewer. So while we may say that an image may or may not achieve a state of equilibrium, we have not said that this image does not move.

Now, I almost said that the image *must* move, that movement is a condition of it being art. But seeing Andreas Gursky's enormous photographs in person, I hesitate: his images are disquietingly still. Some clearly aim for stillness – an empty Prada shelf, for instance. But others, such as those of throngs at a rock concert or the Tokyo Stock exchange, objectively contain movement. There are all the tell-tale signs: blur and sometimes there is what seems to be a double-shot, as if two photographs, taken moments apart, were layered on top of each other. And yet even these images do not move; they won't budge. There is no depth perception; focus and blur have nothing to do with distance and proximity. There is no vantage point, as if a living moment were captured, as if motion begins the moment the shutter releases, or as if the eye of the photographer is in motion, capturing this fleeting event. What McLuhan says of visual space in general can be said of Gursky's photographs in particular: they are "uniform, continuous, and connected." They are a parody of allatonceness. There may be internal differentiation, but there are no points of inflection; nothing happens here. Even in the soccer field, with a player down, there are no events. Indeed, I'd say that a color field painting enjoys more internal differentiation that Gursky's photographs. It's almost as if Gursky works hard to still the movement of life: his image of

Pollock's image makes this explicit as Pollock's lively drips come to a screeching halt under Gursky's watch. And yet "watch" is not the right word for he is altogether absent. There is not vantage point to these images; there are not great shots that he captured. Neither the camera nor the cameraman is in motion: stillness is absolute. I might say that the movement of a Gursky photograph is the non-movement (for it is not a death or even a dearth; the photographs are affirmative).

And so an equilibrium may or may not be achieved, an image may or may not move, but what is it that distinguishes the cinematic image from other moving images? Deleuze tells us that the terms of the "mould" are different. This notion of the mould comes from Bazin. But Bazin sees a very different cinema than Deleuze. For Bazin, cinema is fundamentally representational; hence, he begins with an analysis of the photograph and engages the notion of the mould, an impression of reality. But Deleuze's cinema will never have been representational; as he says, the movement-image is matter, not just a mould-in-flux of matter.

I am not saying a painting and a film are the same; I am not trying to break down the boundaries between them, playing the skeptic, trying to force language to its limits. No, my point is this: the difference lies not in movement per se, not in duration, not in mobility but in the boundaries of movement. There is a difference between a film and a painting or photograph: the frame. What Deleuze says of the respective statures of the moulds is true for the respective statures of the frames; in the cinematic image, there is "a transformation of the [frame] at each moment of the operation." The frame of the cinematic image is in perpetual flux, dissolving, reforming, shifting without pause. The frame of a painting is more-or-less static. Even if we can say that the frame of a painting is in motion – say, Matthew Ritchie's sprawling works that leave the wall, dripping, as it were, onto the floor – the open frame nevertheless enjoys a consistent trajectory: it may be in motion, it may be infinite, but it is one differential equation. A film, on the other hand, shifts equations as it will. Even Calder's mobiles have a boundedness, a frame that is in motion but never dissolves: each mobile is one, albeit elaborate, differential equation.

At times, the frame of a painting next to the endless reframing of a film makes a painting seem stilted, claustrophobic — all the movement of Miró's bird in that tiny space. And yet there is an odd exhilaration at the endless vibration, at the tightly wound flux of a Miró or Klee or Matthew Ritchie. At the zoo one day, I had a revelation while watching the big cats pace in their cramped cages. They were not bored; they were not looking for a way out; they were not frustrated. On the contrary, by moving steadily in their space, the cats transformed the 20-foot cage into a sprawling savannah of infinite horizons. Freedom, they seemed to say, cannot be quantified: this space is infinite because I occupy it, because I *move* in it. This is the thrill of a Klée sketch: within this bounded space, there is infinite movement.

But the swell and vibration of a Klée or Miró or Ritchie will never give way to the continuous modulation of the cinematic image. This is what Deleuze is after from cinema, from the movement-image: becoming, every moment at the limit of its own dissolve, matter in a state of relentless transformation. The bounded, framed image will not know such dissolve; it will never give way to another state. On the contrary, it is this state of movement, this stipulated becoming, *ad infinitum*. It is at once condemned and liberated to repeat itself.

There is a strange kind of condensation to the framed image. I imagine a Matthew Ritchie as an entire film — all the dissolves and transformations — presented within one frame (albeit a frame that is always at its own limit rather than being the container of limits). In some sense, such a painting is film sped up, past the speed of light: his painting is the trace. On the other hand, his painting is a film slowed down so much that transformations endure, never quite come to a head, slur.

This moving framed image, then, is not sequential. It does not relate to a whole but is itself a whole (as Deleuze describes the movement-image: it has a local modulation as well as a modulation of the sequence or series itself). Of course, there are framed images that are part of sequences, Robert Rauschenberg's great set of zipper-attached prints, for example. But the movement or communication between the different images does not constitute the relentless dissolve of the frame as we see in cinema.

Perhaps, then, the movement of the framed image is not the movement-image at all. It may not be an immobile section, its equilibrium may or may not move, but it does not become another image. There is no modulation: it is all bounded fray, a framed set of vibrations, communications, swells. Of course, there are different kinds of movement. Just as Deleuze proffers a topology of cinematic images — the affect-image, the perception-image, the action-image — so there is a topology of framed images: the swell-image, the vibration-image, the hot-image, the cold-image, the wisp-image, etc. A whole set of images, then, each with a dominant mode of movement. There's the fold-image and its subsets: the convex-image, the concave-image, the sharp-turn-image, the micro-pleat-image, the broad-turn-image, etc; the temperature-image, hot to cold, cold to hot, and everything in-between; the speed-image; the rhythm-image, etc... I imagine there are thousands of possible moving-image types.

6

Things Teach

As a thing is its own mode of becoming — a mode of taking up and distributing the world — a thing teaches. It teaches how it goes, how things work here. Each thing is an alien world and it's our job, among other things, to learn its laws, its rules of operation, its tics, twitches, and ways.

A tulip, for instance, offers a way of standing in the world, on one's own without being excessively stern. Grass, meanwhile, instructs us how to be a network of individuals. Certain tequilas teach the way of multiplicity without unity while teaching that sun and leather and grass and heat can play well together in the mouth. The different tastes do not cohere into a common cause, as bourbon often does. Each flavor maintains its local integrity while nonetheless working with the others. Every sip is not only astounding; every sip is an education. *Oh, now I know the world can go like this!*

Here's a list of things uni — raw sea-urchin gonads — has taught me:

1. All is becoming
2. The most discrete domains house infinite variation
3. Limits need be neither hard nor fast
4. I should embrace ambiguity
5. Self-possession comes through flexibility
6. Experience is everything — life is a *how*, not a *what*
7. The skank of life is often delicious
8. Be discerning — a life well vetted is a life well lived
9. Eat the world
10. Let the world eat you

To the immanent reader, everything offers its own science, its own knowledge. A thing is a pedagogy. The world brims with different ways of going, different ways of making sense of the world. We don't just heed human ways. In fact, perhaps we need inhuman ways to teach us fundamentally different ways of going. We need the saguaro cactus to teach us to go slowly, boldly in the sun, just as we need the oak to teach us how to be majestic and generous. We need the flow of the river to teach us speed and cooperation with the land. We need clouds to learn to drift softly; cats for their relentless attentiveness; dogs for their loyalty; the wind for its vigor and swirl. Everything is a possibility. And even if we don't go like this or that — like a cat, like a cloud, like a river — we can take pieces of these becomings, we can come to know the world more intimately, we can be stretched and folded and extended. We can learn to go, and to go interestingly, to go curiously, to go delightfully: to go well.

This is all to say that reading need not be a confirmation of what you already know. It can be a forging of worlds to come, of things you don't know, of things you didn't even know were possible. To read a text is to dwell in a new world with its own inevitably peculiar laws of operation. To see Francis Bacon paintings is to discover a strange and disconcerting physiology where flesh is tenuously tethered to bone. To read Nabokov is to be denied conceptual grounding, to be carried along a linguistic erotic play that refuses to resolve, explain, or stop. If an exemplary reader scans the world looking for things that he can fit into his world — *Oh, that's deconstructive! That's Deleuzian! That's Buddhist!* — the immanent reader discovers alien worlds, new ways of going, of operating, of being and becoming.

7

Good and Bad vs. Right and Wrong

There may be infinite readings of this or that text but there are still good and bad readings. A good reading is creative. Things once familiar become refreshingly unfamiliar. The reader is a progenitor of the uncanny as habit falls away and a thing experienced hundreds of times suddenly comes into focus as if for the very first time. Few things exhilarate the way a good reading does. A fine and fresh distinction or well-placed reversal infuses the banal with vitality, the quotidian with wonder, the dead with life.

The reversal is a great reading move. In the reversal, expectation and assumptions are, well, reversed. Nietzsche, for instance, loves reversals. Christian morality, he argues, is built on hate and resentment cloaked in the passive-aggressive stance of love. Christian belief in God is nihilistic, a belief in nothing rather than a living through of life — a devastating reversal as Christian love becomes hate and faith becomes nihilism.

Or take Gabriel Kolko's essay on the creation of the USDA that claimed that the USDA and its dispensation of approval — those assuring gradations of meat — were *not* born of consumer advocacy but were in fact a foil of the meat industry, an industry suffering due to Upton Sinclair's *The Jungle* which exposed the grotesqueries of meat-packing. The USDA, then, was not only *not* there to protect my fellow citizens and me; *it was in fact an elaborate abuse of governmental ethos, a ploy to move product, a product which may very well be harmful to the very citizens the USDA was nominally formed to protect.*

In both these readings, expectations are reversed. But it's not as simple as turning something upside-down, flipping from hot to cold. No, in the very act of reversal, the very terms are redistributed. Expectations are flipped on their head, for sure. And the person reading Nietzsche or Kolko finds her experiences being flipped all around. What was once taken for granted is seen anew, radically anew.

Sometimes, these readings take surprising turns. I remember being in college and hearing the historian Carroll Smith-Rosenberg lecture on the culture of the faint Victorian woman. Expecting to hear the tale of patriarchic oppression (which at the time seemed interesting and familiar to my decidedly uninteresting and familiar mind), my body readied itself for confirmation, for that nod — *Yes, aren't we all in this together?* — a communal blind spot, or what we might call common sense.

But the tale I was to hear snapped me right to attention. The feminine assumption of weakness, it turns out, was not solely a means by which men subjugated women. No, the faintness of Victorian women was in fact a strategy by which a woman could a) avoid the toiling duties of housekeeper and hostess; and b) if institutionalized, be with other women. A feminine posture of weakness and the entire medical culture surrounding it was *not* just another example of men keeping women down; *it was in fact a feminine strategy of survival and pleasure.* (Reversals demand italics — they make the words themselves careen.)

Now take *The History of Sex, Volume 1*. Michel Foucault argues that the discourse of the repression and liberation of sexuality is part of the same discourse of power: repression does not repress and liberation does not liberate. They are both constitutive of a will to power that endlessly articulates sex and rigorously controls it. For Foucault, the very notion that sex is something that can be repressed and hence liberated is part of the system of control that is built on the logic of the depth: the soul must be mined to its deep, dark recesses.

How does Foucault reach this conclusion? He spent days, weeks, months in the archives and found a veritable explosion of documents speaking, in one way or another, about sex. Sex clearly was not repressed. And yet we walk around speaking as though it were, as though it were in need of liberation. Foucault, then, looks at what we say *and* what we do *and* the relationship between the two

These, I am arguing, are good readings. Rather than taking the world at its word, these readings heed the performance of the text at hand and then put it all together in a surprising way, flipping the thing's own claims on its head, which in turn creates new architectures of becoming. A good reading does not confirm the known; it spins the elements into new shapes, new possibilities so we see the thing anew, as if for the very first time.

Of course, one doesn't need to reverse in order to render the world uncanny. Take Kierkegaard's reading of Plato. When I borrow from Kierkegaard and say that Socrates proffers a way of life (irony), not a rigid philosophy (Platonism with its Forms), I am not reversing Plato. Rather, I am offering an alternate way to read Plato's texts, how they *behave*. In any case, the goal of the reader is to fold, pleat, spin, cut, shape the world in some way that does not seek to confirm *the known* but rather seeks *the unknown*. To read well is literally an *adventure*, a forward-looking propriety, a thing being made in the very act of reading. As Steve Zissou declares at the end of Wes Anderson's film *The Life Aquatic*, "This is an adventure."

This is really a matter of one's posture in the world, how one stands towards things, towards experience. Do you seek to *recognize* the world? Or *(re)create* it? Of course, we often seek to confirm what we know. This is not a bad thing. On the contrary, it is necessary. This is how we organize our world. But when I come to a book or art or politics or sometimes just a glass of tequila, I want to see it anew; I want to spin it into new shapes and new modes of living. I want to be led astray of myself, taken somewhere new and exciting. I want the world to shimmer and gleam.

Of course, not all readings fare so well. Søren Kierkegaard

claims that so-called Christianity mis-reads Jesus and His Testament. The Church, Kierkegaard tells us, picks up where the Gospels leave off, *after* Jesus has risen. But for Kierkegaard, Christianity — and faith in particular — is a matter of reckoning the *life* of Jesus. A poor, skinny Jew stands before you and claims to be the eternal God. Believe him or don't: that is the struggle of faith. A historically specific person claims to be eternal; it's absurd. And yet it is precisely on the strength of this absurdity that a true Christian finds faith. To premise one's faith on a Jesus who has risen is, for Kierkegaard, to miss Christianity all together. After all, Jesus' words come while he is alive. So Kierkegaard asks us to be *contemporaneous* with the text, with the disciplines, to hear Jesus' words as if they were spoken, while He was still alive and the burden of faith is on you. It's not that the Church is wrong per se; rather, it's that the Church reads the Gospels *badly.*

Ted Morgan entitles his biography of William S. Burroughs *Literary Outlaw.* Few would find this title surprising; indeed, it seems appropriate. After all, Burroughs is the bad boy of literature, eschewing plot, consistency of voice, character development, and perhaps every other literary convention. This reading *works.*

But it's not terribly interesting. Burroughs, reading himself, takes issue with this characterization of his work: "To be an outlaw you must first have a base in law to reject and get out of. I never had such a base." (ME 7) That is to say, to read Burroughs as an outlaw is to read him as *reacting* to the laws of literature rather than *(re)inventing* them.

A good reading is *uncanny*, taking the familiar and making it unfamiliar so you at once know and don't know the thing. To see things, to think things, to sense things that you didn't even know existed, to experience turns of thought, insights and twists, nuances and qualifications: a good reading is exhilarating. To read a good reading of a film or painting or book is akin to seeing

Rafael Nadal work his opponent to one side of the court before delivering a drop shot to the other side; it's akin to watching Michael Jordan penetrate a defense, stop, turn, jump in the air backwards and sink a basket without a hint of rim. A good reading is athletic.

A reading can't really be wrong — there is no code to be deciphered, no truth awaiting behind or within the words. The author will not come to deliver the Word from on high. Nor will the critic or the professor. All there are are different readings.

And yet a reading can be out of bounds. To say that *Moby Dick* is a tale of Soviet oppression is just plain silly. And, I suppose, we can say it's wrong. Such a reading can be violent to a text, making it bend in uncomfortable ways. So perhaps rather than saying a reading is wrong, we can say a reading is distasteful? Unethical? Foul — as in baseball? Yes, I like "foul" because it is at once ethical, aesthetic, and fair. There may be no *proof* that a reading is right but there is *evidence*— a foul pole of a sort. To read something demands attention, an accounting for what's *there*, for what's happening. It is empirical.

And then there are plain old *bad* readings of things. These are readings that may very well be in bounds but that are bad for any number of reasons. A bad reading may make the thing less interesting, quashing its multivalences, such as the writing on the wall in the museum at the Philip Guston show that reduced Guston's work to a symptom of his childhood. Or calling Burroughs an "outlaw" when he really is an outlaw of both the law and the outlaws. And, to be fair to Ted Morgan, I think this is how we can read his title: Burroughs is not an outlaw per se, he is always already outside the law.

A bad reading may just be obvious, the reader not really doing anything at all but echoing that which has already declared itself. An example might be when a reader reads Nietzsche and claims that Nietzsche does not believe in truth. That's a bad reading because, well, Nietzsche's texts say they do not believe in, or ascribe to, truth as a value in and of itself. A *good* reading would tease out the rhetorical nuance of Nietzsche's claim, perhaps show how truth functions for him — as not just something that is or isn't but as something that operates within an elaborate will-to-power and how that might impact what it is to be a reader of Nietzsche. In any case, a good reading does not reduce or state the obvious: it sheds light on places you didn't even know existed — as perhaps they didn't before this reading.

Example 3: Reading Burroughs: The Gunk and Flow of the World

To read Burroughs is to discover new laws that legislate a baseless, or at least multi-based, universe. His is a world of viscous flux, a world that flows in a syrupy, *gunky* way. Bodies overflow — not with blood, which is mostly aqueous, too even — but with semen and shit, with entrails and ooze. Bodies distend and bloat; they reach their limits, engorged with their own creeping desires, relentlessly excessive and dehiscent. Hard-ons pop up relentlessly; piles get caught in the wheels; people shit themselves. Death hovers, the world ever bordering at its own limit. Meanwhile, immortality hovers as well, the Western Lands offering its own set of limits. Burroughs returns often to strangulation and its accompanying production: erection, ejaculation, an evacuation of the bladder and bowels. Borders drip: minds meld, bodies conjoin and morph, time swirls. His language performs this. Alternately sparse and baroque, sweet and savage, deadpan noir and gay dream, his words stumble into each other as periods and commas give way to the force of an undulating universe.

The flux of the world is relentless but is not steady. It is a world defined by various speeds and consistencies, diverse rhythms and shapes: objects move and interact at rates particular to them. As Kim Carson advises those wannabe gunfighters in *The Place of Dead Roads*, "Take *Your* Time," the time particular to you. Of course, if the other guy's time is faster, you're done for. Each thing has a way to it or what Burroughs calls "tThe Mmark Iinside" with its "Aalgebra of nNeed": each Mmark houses a need, desires and instincts, the 'x' in its equation of life. For the junk addict, it's junk; for the backroom capitalist, it's greed and money. Clearly, these different equations entail different speeds, different worldly affects and effects.

Burroughs' prose approaches the filmic in putting forth such a plethora of rhythms and possibilities in the same scene. (Burroughs admired film for its formal advances in performing synchronicity; his writing often explicitly apes cinema as he cops the language of film — zoom, pan, cut.) A patient squirms beneath Dr. Benway's arbitrary incisions; a nurse earnestly assists, questioning the doctor's actions without outrage; Benway utters dicta and observations at once astute and absurd; body parts slop about; Benway tells outlandish tales of other doctors' techniques. The effect is complex and multiple: vaudevillian, satiric, hilarious, absurd, grotesque all at once — and yet at different rates and in different ways. The slopping intestines are viscerally gross; Benway's story of a doctor prancing into the operating room hurling his knife towards the patient acts as a cartoonish interlude: we see the doctor pirouetting into the room, a dandy with a scalpel. But we also see Benway cutting up the patient; we smell the detritus, hear the slop of organs and blood. Meanwhile, the nurse's earnestness does not ground the scene — she's no Ed McMahon. Her presumably sane posture amid the insanity is perhaps the most insane presence, a steady hum propelling the whole closer to madness. When the sanest person in the room accepts this madness as if it were normal, all normalcy, ground, and sanity has gone by the wayside.

While Burroughs' world is kinetic, it is not a digital kinetics, the frenzy of ones and zeroes. His world is not geometric. It's a calculus, punctuated with variable curves which move at variable speeds, at times whipping along the linear velocity of a bullet or oozing to the rhythm of brains emptied from their skulls. If we were to visually graph Burroughs' writing, it might look like a Matthew Ritchie painting. Or perhaps Burroughs' world is closer to the elastic madness of *Loony Tunes*: Burroughs, the Chuck Jones of literature.

Bugs Bunny is the consummate Burroughs hero. Bugs is a keen reader of his circumstances, always at the ready with an endless bag of tricks, able to slip in and out of trouble at will, and with no agenda other than going about his business. Bugs is not a moral rabbit.

Burroughs' heroes — an amalgamation of himself, Bugs, Denton Welch, and Sam Spade, among others — are navigators, readers of a world that careens on the verge of chaos. They succeed because they know how things go, "moving now with speed and precision as every object slides into its assigned place" (Burroughs, PDR 53). In "DE," Burroughs outlines the method and discipline of learning the world, of mastering its rhythms, of moving harmoniously with its demands: repeat the same gesture, focus on it, move towards efficient doing, the right amount of energy for each task: DE, do easy.

Like El Hombre Invisible himself, or Bugs for that matter, Burroughs' heroes slip into the gaps of perception, morphing as the situation demands, never afraid to don the guise of their enemies and armed with a variety of stratagems to infiltrate forbidden places. To survive the viscosity of the universe, a syrup riddled with waves of stupidity, bigotry, and unabashed greed, one must cling lightly to principles, be impeccably poised for whatever may arise, and always — *always* — be cool: "What's up, doc?"

And mind your own fucking business — which may be the sole dictum of the Burroughs ethic. And which is deceptively complex: to mind one's own business amidst a universe in flux, a universe ripe with collisions, is no simple task. To mind one's own business is not a call to solipsism; it entails a posture at once participatory and self-possessed. It is a matter of politesse, of considered negotiation.

The cut-up method demands such politesse. In the cut-up technique, Burroughs takes snippets of writing (his own, a newspaper headline, a Shakespeare sonnet, whatever), tosses them in a pile, more or less, and pulls them out (or folds them together at surprising angles), thereby creating prose. The cut-up repeats the world of collision and chance as prose from diverse sources, moods, and times meet at unexpected angles. It is Burroughs' job as writer to navigate these collisions, to make a sense of them, to propitiously consume them, a considered negotiation in the midst of world bereft of care and consideration yet overflowing with powerful forces that drive action.

For Burroughs, politeness is an effective mode of steering one's way through a crowded world, a strategy of politesse. Indeed, for all of his outlandish claims and sordid prose, Burroughs usually conducted himself as a gentleman. Politeness maintains a distance while interacting; it is a collision that respects the borders of all parties, accounting for others while letting them be: "Excuse me," and shuffle on by.

And yet amidst the frenzy of this world unmoored, a world of conflict and relentless negotiation, flourish moments of grace, what Burroughs calls "cuteness": cats, lemurs, raccoons, skunks. For Burroughs, cuteness is at once ethical and aesthetic, marking a juncture at which the world contentedly coalesces. Cuteness is not an ideal for which to strive but is a moment of grace within the teeming grotesqueries and stresses of worldly flux. If the plight of being human is the relentless negotiation, cute creatures make no trying demands: they are loving without being needy, self-possessed without being righteous. Dogs are never cute because they know the difference between right and wrong; dogs are moral creatures, capable of self-righteousness — they can't just mind their own fucking business. But the cat is capable of supreme indifference while simultaneously expressing love. *The Cat Inside* is Burroughs' great eulogy for cuteness in general and cats in particular.

8

Generosity

Immanent reading is an encounter between at least two things. And, more likely, it is an encounter between multiple multiplicities, a juncture of bodies interacting in diverse ways. Reading, then, is necessarily a matter of how things go together, of the very terms of engagement in this world. Reading is a matter of ethics.

In taking up a thing, there is always the risk of violence. People force texts to do all sorts of terrible things. Just look at what the Nazis did to Nietzsche. Think of all the Oedipal readings of David Lynch, the biographic readings of Burroughs — how condescending to reduce Burroughs to a product of his times, his anger to his homosexuality! It's rude — not to Burroughs (although also to Burroughs) but to his texts.

And it's disrespectful. It doesn't allow the text to speak, to do what it wants to do. To read something in light of a pre-given concept or genre or life is to reduce, if not erase, the vitality of a thing. It's the same when one reduces a child to his parents and say the kid is only an example, a derivative, of the parents. But isn't it obvious that the child demands our respect? Demands that we read him on his own terms and not solely as something derived from his parents? To read something, or at least to read it well, demands respect — not respect for the canon but respect for life.

And a certain generosity. Why generosity? Because to read well you have to come to the thing assuming that whatever comes is the best possible thing. A good reader does not look for how a text *fails* but for how it *succeeds* — in becoming itself. You may loathe the text or the things it claims but that doesn't make it a failure per se.

This is not a moral imperative and reading is not a *moral* exercise. It's an *ethical* exercise. There is no code, no set of rules. There is only a very strange and beautiful principle: be generous. It's strange because it is a principle that determines nothing but rather lets a thing determine itself. Generosity is a principle of (in)difference, maximizing diversity, plenitude, multiplicity. And it is a beautiful principle because it only wants, only asks for, what is great.

After all, why spend time with something that's not great? To point out the flaws of something usually shuts the world down. It speaks to an unhealthy instinct — complaining, saying no. It's an odd expenditure of energy, like revenge. If you don't like it, let it be and pick up something that drives your vitality. Does this mean one can't write critically of a book, film, work of art, other human being? No, of course not. It is important, even essential, that we say *no* to certain texts, to certain things, that we articulate precisely why this or that text creates certain problems. But it is the manner in which we say no, the manner in which we critique, that matters.

In *Leaves of Grass*, Walt Whitman gives us the great Yes-saying. He says yes to everything — to every leaf, person, smell, moment. He is voracious, exuberant, joyous through and through. Nietzsche, too, is a great Yes-sayer. "My formula for greatness in man," writes Nietzsche in *Ecce Homo*, "is *amor fati*: the fact that a man wishes nothing to be different, either in front of him or behind him, or for all eternity." This is the ultimate affirmative claim: love fate, love everything that happens to you — sickness, sadness, banality, joy — and wish it no other way. But Nietzsche, unlike Whitman, says *no* to all sorts of things — to coffee and alcohol, to Christian morality and German anti-Semitism, to pity and to the herd. But this is different than the No-saying of the nihilists who say no to life. When Nietzsche says no, he is saying yes to his own becoming, to his own constitution, to his own intestinal health (which was poor). Sometimes, we affirm ourselves when we say no. It all depends on *how* we do it.

Occasionally, we don't like something for interesting reasons, for surprising reasons. I disliked *Wall-E* for being too humanistic in a bourgeois fashion while it is precisely this bourgeois humanism and its will to ownership that is the cause of the planet's decimation in the first place. When I published this reading on a popular film blog, it was met with anger and distress; the blog didn't invite me back. But what interested me was not that I liked or didn't like the film. What interested me, what engaged my attention, were the surprising reasons why I didn't like it. That is to say, I enjoyed thinking about why I didn't like it — the *thinking* was interesting even if the *film* was not.

Generosity a) assumes the best possible thing from the text — it assumes the text is "right" rather than contradicting itself; and b) is the will of the reader to amplify the complexity, the beauty, the interest of the text. For instance, in *Phaedrus*, Socrates often says one thing — say, writing makes us forget by externalizing our memory — and does another: Socrates, who does not write, forgets all sorts of things throughout the dialog. Do we say, then, that Socrates, or Plato, contradicts himself? Or, instead, do we ask: What is the relationship between this saying and this doing? What happens when Socrates says one thing and does another? This is to say, we assume the best from the text.

The immanent reader is not interested in passing judgment, on saying whether a thing is good or bad, giving a film or book or person that thumbs-up or thumbs-down. The immanent reader makes his judgment by deciding to spend time with something. At which point, his reading seeks not to judge but to amplify, to magnify, to explore and discover, to follow *how* a thing goes. You may not even like the thing at all; that's irrelevant. What matters is that you are capable of following it.

What matters is that you are willing to give up your body, to lend your emotional and physical state to the thing. To let the film or book or painting or flower or other person move you, to make an impression on the text that is you. Just as we let a chair shape our posture, we let a thing inflect us, shape our moods and bodies. Being generous, we let the thing play across us, impress upon us.

Generously, an immanent reading follows the multiple threads and trajectories of a text, exploring and amplifying its manifold dimensions.

9

Power, or Saying No

There are limits to a reader's generosity. To go well with something can mean *not* acquiescing to its terms. After all, the world brims with the cruel, the mad, the vampiric. And a reader must tend to himself — to his health and vitality — as well as to the world.

Reading the social at times demands indifference, dissimulation, even conflict. Take walking down the street in any major American city. One is assaulted by oblivious or selfish drivers, the diseased, the distracted, the downright mean. The immanent reader does not have to be generous to all the demands of these encounters. No, reading in today's frantic world demands a wide set of tactics and tools. Politeness is one effective one, a social protocol that maintains distance, allowing both you the others to maintain their respective privacy while still noting them, accounting for them.

Work is one place where unadulterated generosity — meeting the event on its terms — can be disastrous for one's health. One aspect of power is to try and determine the very way we not only discuss things but the way in which we think about things. So we feel guilty if we're late to work — *despite the fact that we spend 50, 60, 70 hours a week there!* We feel guilty if we text with friends online while at our work desks. Our very emotional self-assessments are penetrated by the insidious and pervasive discourses of power.

Reading things well does not mean we need to succumb to all conditions put to us. Sometimes — perhaps often — reading the way of things demands a certain dissimulation or indifference. In *The Practice of Everyday Life*, Michel de Certeau proffers a ruse — *la perruque* — as a way of reading *with* the terms power puts forth. *La perruque* entails looking as though one is working while actually putting the resources of capital to use for oneself — writing a novel when you're supposed to be writing a tagline, building a rocket for yourself instead of a car for Ford. Obviously, if you never write the tagline or build the car, you'll be fired, lose your ability to pay rent, be tossed aside. Reading well hence entails heeding what needs to get done, putting on the proper look of diligence and mirth and then quietly going about one's own business. *La perruque* is not a going-*against* but a mode of going-*with*. Tyler Durden's professional experience, especially as a caterer, pushes this to a limit.

The good reader sizes up the situation and makes the most of it. This is true whether reading a book, a film, a person, a martini glass. If you find yourself eating a meal that makes you sick, you stop eating. So it is with a book or film or art: turn away, put it down. But in the social, one cannot always walk away so readily. This is why when reading the social, and particularly when enmeshed in a power scenario, one must resort to the ruse in order to make the most of things. Confronting your boss by calling him an incompetent moron is rarely a keen reading tactic — if you don't end up losing your job, you will make the everyday intolerable. Of course, there is a certain delight in calling out one's incompetent boss. And, at times, it might be the best possible thing to do, a good reading of a given situation.

But there is a beautiful kind of mastery that entails making the dysfunction of the social — and of work in particular — productive. This means abandoning one's principles of honesty in all situations. It may mean ridding oneself of dignity, at least in appearances. It may mean sitting there and letting your moron boss think he's the smartest guy in the room while you know — you *know* — that's not true. It means nodding and smiling — "Yes, of course, I'm on it!" — while quietly doing the things that make you happy. Take the check, tend to yourself, and scurry on out of there.

Reading the way of things is complex and is not simply a matter of succumbing. It is a matter of *negotiating* a calculus of indifference, passion, health, life. What kind of expenditure — personal, financial, spiritual — will such-and-such demand? While you may cling to your principles, this doesn't mean you need to announce your adherence. You can look like you're one of the crowd when you're anything but.

This does not mean one should always eat proverbial shit. There may be very good reasons — revolutionary or personal — for announcing your feelings. And, sometimes, this announcement may be dramatic, extreme, confrontational, even violent. But always ask yourself: What is the play here? How can I make sense of this situation so as to maximize it — not for the company or the boss or even for yourself per se but for the good of the world, for beauty and grace, for the moment and what it seems to be demanding? This is not a call to unbridled selfishness. It is a call to the complexity of reading the social, of making sense of this exceedingly complicated world.

And, of course, this is not algebra; the reader isn't solving for X. There is no one right, best thing to do. The situation is multiple for all parties at all times. You are Pi in which no one knows the next number until it's happened.

Going with the world is not an abandonment of oneself — that would be going *for*. And the immanent reader does not go *for* his work or his principles. He goes *with* them. He enjoys a complex constitution of desires, loves, limits, propensities, metabolisms. To read well means maximizing the event of which the reader is constitutive. To completely abandon oneself is not to read well; it is to be a lackey, a disciple, a slave.

Let's consider the Pixar film *Toy Story* for a moment. The film gives us two relationships to things. On the one hand, there's Andy who plays with his toys as they were "meant" to be played with — the cowboy acts like a cowboy, the astronaut like an astronaut. Now, Andy does take some license but the terms of his

71

play always conform to some traditional narrative from which these toys were born.

And then there's Sid. Sid does not think, for one moment, that he has to obey his toys or the terms prescribed by their meta-narratives. Sid looks at toys and sees play, combination, the head of this one should go on that one, this foot should come out the ear, a hole needs to be drilled there.

Can we consider either one of these an immanent reader? Andy seems to read things on their own terms while Sid flagrantly disregards all such terms. But just because a toy is prescribed to be used a certain way doesn't mean that is the limit of what that toy can do. Following a prescription is not reading (although it may be; it all depends on the situation). Is there an immanent reading in Sid's toy surgery? Perhaps. He may be more of an artist than a reader, creating new things from the scraps of the old. But, then again, he may be maximizing each toy, seeing how Buzz Lightyear really does want to fly, and even die; how the baby head doesn't want to be stuck on the same old baby body but wants some cool, metal legs; and perhaps, in melting his plastic army men, Sid is following the plasticity so prevalent in said figures. Perhaps. In any case, Sid is no lackey.

Reading the way of things may be generous but it's not an abandonment of one's way of going.

10

Reading amidst the Social

The social moves fast, enmeshing the reader in its tendrils even before the reader has arrived on the scene. Alas, as a reader, you are always already on the scene. You are prefigured before you've even entered the room — your gender, race, class, your place in the sexual and social hierarchy. As Althusser says, we are hailed even before we're born: *Hey you!* And we look.

You're in a bar. You look around. You catch someone's eyes. She has some look on her face, some expression of her history and her now — a look of fatigue, befuddlement, boredom, urgency, fear, delight. This expression is, of course, never just one of those things but is an undulating set of affects. Once you look at her, this expression changes, however imperceptibly. This, in turn, affects your expression. Which, in turn, inflects hers. This is an infinite circuit that is crisscrossed by any number of other circuits — social, historical, cultural, physical, sexual, circumstantial (noise level, public events, your respective group of friends, your need to use the bathroom). Together, you are making the world.

Obviously, the terms of reading the event change depending on where and who you are. A young African-American male dressed in a sweatshirt and baggy pants and a white man dressed in a suit are read differently and hence must read differently.

And it's quite different if you're reading a book or work of art. But, as Henri Bergson might say, this difference is not one of kind but of speed and degree of intensity. That is, when we read books, art, and films, we are enmeshed in the event of reading just as we are in the social. We are implicated. But the speed with which this happens, and our time of reaction, is usually much slower.

The point, among others, is this: as a reader, you are constitutive of the reading event. You do not have the privilege of standing outside the fray; you *are* the fray — or at least part of it. Whatever you do inflects the whole, and vice-versa. This makes any reading complex but it makes reading in the social exponentially complex as glances, gestures, words are exchanged at near-infinite speeds, all amidst the relentlessly fluctuating desires and bodies of people.

This is the starting point of Gonzo journalism: join the fray, constitute the fray, be constituted by the fray as a way of knowing the world. The Gonzo journalist stands amongst his subjects, even getting stomped by some Angels. There is a knowledge to be had here, a knowledge that is different than the knowledge that comes from standing back. The one who writes about the concert from the balcony offers a different knowledge than the one who writes about it from the mosh pit. Neither is privileged; each offers its perspective, its own kind of knowing. But, in saying that, we shift the fundamental terms of knowing. To know is not to be objective, to stand back. To know is to reckon from your perspective. "We must begin *wherever we are* and the thought of the trace, which cannot not take the scent into account, has already taught us that it was impossible to justify a point of departure absolutely. *Wherever we are*: in a text wherever we already believe ourselves to be" (Derrida, OG 162).

How does one go with this great teeming? It is so easy to be evacuated, at the whim of the flux as your phone rings, texts stream in, emails ding, your friends and co-workers and family greet and holler and before long you are so thoroughly enmeshed in replying that you are incapable of actually making sense of things. You become so sliced and diced by networks that you vanish all together in one great *whoosh* of beeps and blips.

Another option is to become the master, the expert, who plugs all the whims and vicissitudes of the quotidian into the same set schema over and over again. Rather than being at the mercy of every blip and bleep, this expert turns every blip and bleep into the service of his schema, his order of things. This expert is not swayed by the winds but stands firm and sure.

Of course, we are all some amalgamation of these two — sometimes finding ourselves caught in a dense web of networks; other times, parrying the power of the now by relying on our familiar ways of understanding the world. But I want to suggest that there is a third place: standing amidst the flurry, leaning neither into the flux nor back from it, a posture of poise.

11

Poise

The immanent reader enjoys a posture of poise, at once resigned *and* active, ready *and* reposed. This reader goes with a thing without totally abandoning himself. Picture the surfer: he turns into the maelstrom for his power while holding steady unto himself. The surfer is poised, going *with* the ocean.

This *going with* is not immediate. Or, rather, it is not solely immediate. To read is not to engage a pure nowness. But neither is it to let the past, or the future, dictate the terms of the engagement. The reader cannot shake his history, his experiences, everything he knows and enjoys and loves and hates. The reader is rich in his own history, his memory, his becoming. Or, better, the reader *is* — *becomes* — his history. To go with something is a complex equation of bodies rich in history. Which is to say, poise is not nowness; it's attentiveness and willingness to go with while still going as one goes.

Have you ever watched a person in the act of making sense of something? One of the side effects of contemporary American coffee-shop culture — everyone sitting in front of a laptop — is that we are privy to people's once-private modes of intellectual reckoning. Look around one of these coffee shops. Single out one person and just watch. Watch the tics and leans, the furrows and taps, the sighs and grunts. This is a body at work, digesting, processing, productively consuming. Ideas move our bodies just as our bodies move ideas. This is sense-surfing, riding the waves of sense, turning into this tube of sense, cruising there, occasionally getting pummeled by the tumult.

Posture is a matter of ethics, of how one reckons the world. This is what's at stake, what we talk about when we talk about reading: How do you stand towards, and with, the world?

The immanent reader's posture is at once sure and precarious, set in place and always moving with what comes. He takes all of his experiences, all his capabilities, and puts them in play with this thing before him. And soon that thing is mixing this way and that with all the other things that make up our reader.

A reading, then, necessarily differs from reader to reader. One who has read dramatic plays extensively will read Plato differently than one who has read philosophy extensively. Both of these will differ from a reader who has only ever read Archie comics or *The New York Times* or tweets upon tweets. None of these readers is privileged — not the philosopher, not the comic-book reader, not our theater enthusiast or prolific tweeter. They all bring what they bring. Plato's *Phaedrus* finds its way, takes its place, in these particular networks that forge this or that reader. And then there is the particular way a body goes. One reader digests quickly and makes connections along conceptual trajectories while another lets the language linger and finds much in syntax, rhythm, and rhyme. We make sense differently. A reader brings himself to the reading. But in order to read he must actively put aside cliché and habit. He must work to look at this thing fresh. He must be open but not empty, receptive but not passive, active but not dictatorial.

The reader does not begin reading from an empty place. There is no absolute origin, some pure zero from which we're sprung. When a reader takes up a text, his reading has always already begun. This is not a bad thing. This is not to be avoided or shunned. This is what the hermeneutic philosopher, Hans-Georg Gadamer, calls *prejudice*. But this is not license for the reader to meander and indulge his deepest, darkest secrets — although these deepest, darkest secrets are always at work informing every reading to a greater or lesser degree.

The reader begins reading. This beginning is multiple. It has prongs, trajectories, tendrils — a book has a title, a chapter scheme, a rhythm of prose, word selection, characters, story, asides. A painting has color, mood, figure, mark, size, scale, speed. Part of a text penetrates the reader; another part is so much nonsense; in other parts, the reader can jump into the text and frolic. Reading is a relentless negotiation, sorting, assembling, splaying, folding, pleating, parrying, ignoring, reducing, amplifying.

The reader approaches a thing as if it were an unknown, with a certain and complex kind of stupidity: he assumes the text and nothing else. Before this text there's no history or genre, there's no such thing as people or religion or gender or earth — at least not for sure. Perhaps it's better to say there are always multiple and different histories and genres, different kinds of people, religions, genders, and earths and this text in his hands offers its people, genders, religions, physics, genres, histories. Each thing (re)creates the world, recasts history and language and all the laws of behavior. The reader picks the thing up and asks: How does it construe things? How does this thing go with the world, make sense of other things? How does it do what it does? A thing whispers (or screams or deadpans or hollers) its science. The reader, attuned to the way of the way, lets each thing determine its own way — which is always a way of taking up other things. (Picture the surfer looking for her set: she notes the waves, the wind, the other surfers, what's happening now as well as the ways she's experienced waves before — the ways of waves.)

Gilles Deleuze infiltrates the texts he reads. This can make reading his books disconcerting. It's as if he crawls in the skin of the text, into its digestive and circulatory systems, and from within begins to express himself and live. The reader of Deleuze hence often feels like the conversation is already in session; one joins in with Deleuze, just as Deleuze joins in with Nietzsche, Leibniz, Spinoza, cinema, whom or whatever. Deleuze does not introduce that which he's reading, as if he ever stood outside of them. His books begin mid-stride, the reading always already begun. He might call this the middle. The reader of Deleuze must learn to keep up. A blurring of identity occurs as a kind of text-Deleuze figure becomes the author. Or perhaps it is better to say there is a shared skin.

Or one could say that reading Leibniz, Deleuze and Leibniz harmonize together with baroque grace; reading Spinoza, Deleuze rides the broom along Spinoza's wind of a One with infinite attributes; reading Nietzsche, Deleuze repeats Nietzsche in forging a constellation of concepts and characters (rather than a system). Each thinker demands his own rhythm: *Nietzsche and Philosophy* is a fragmented set of readings oriented around Nietzsche's proliferation of concepts, ideas, and figures. *The Fold: Leibniz and the Baroque* is marbled in a baroque vein as examples stream through other examples, origami running alongside differential calculus running alongside Paul Klee's convex curves. In order to reckon Spinoza's dual registers — Spinoza writes in parallel modes — Deleuze engages Spinoza twice, *Expressionism* and *Practical Philosophy*. The one breezes along, the other labors, tacking into the winds of logic and argument (thanks to the geometric method).

Reading involves great personal discipline, a fine attunement to the gesticulations not only of the thing but of one's own body, one's reactive system. The senses must be keen — all the senses, not just the five we know so well. The reader must be willing to go into uncharted territory, to field events and effects heretofore unknown (at least to the reader), to wrestle the strangest of concepts, the most subtle of emotional demands.

In the great *Poetical Dictionary*, the poet and sophist Lohren Green reads words. He stumbles on a word, or is drawn to it or it to him; the word infiltrates his mind and body, birthing investigative tendrils, and he asks: What is the rhythm of the word? What are its meanings? What is its etymology? How does it do what it does? Green assesses all these things — meanings, timbre, connotation and denotation, etymology, the manner in which a word gathers itself up, its history, its possibilities of use, its oral and aural demands, its semantic echoes, projections, and traces, its grammatical insinuations and implications. "Serendipity" skips along; "that" performs the quiver of darts that it is; "oyster" is nebulously oceanic: "acrobat" plants its landing. As the reader of the word, Green turns this way and that until a system, discontinuities and all, emerges. Green surfs the sense of a word.

A reader discovers sense, not just meaning. And this sense mingles with the sense of the reader, necessarily. Green wonders if his reckoning of foreplay doesn't go far enough, if his poise leans too far forward, if his glee is too boyish. But he will never find the purity of the word; its sense will never reveal itself once and for all. All a reader has is his generosity and athleticism, his ability to follow the swells.

Making sense can be scary as it is uncertain what will come. The beginning of a movie is an anxious moment. There's a bombardment of signs as a world is constructed before our eyes. It is a swift composition (a novel or painting is more luxuriously paced); within mere minutes a universe of characters and their inter-relations is established, usually without any meta-narrative or explanation. As I begin to stitch it all together, a subtle panic lurks: What if sense never emerges? What if I can't figure out what's going on?

And there is always that one person — perhaps a friend, perhaps someone else in the theater — who cannot wait for the shapes to emerge, for the sense to coalesce: *Who's that guy? Why's he doing that?* These questions become infuriating nudges, inspiring a visceral rage: despite my predominantly passive incli-nations, I want to cause bodily harm to the failed hermeneut, friend or not. A blind madness emerges. To make sense of things is to live. For someone to ask me to make sense for him is to ask me to live for him. But I'm already busy living my own life, making my own sense of the world. Hence, a primal urge to eliminate the creature who wants my life.

To read is to wrestle, an encounter of bodies, at least mine and the text's. Sense is not guaranteed.

A reader does not necessarily follow a text *wherever* it goes. Or at least not precisely. Disjunctures, displeasures, caesuras, gaps, twisted pleats, and unexpected reversals all work to define a reader's engagement. A reader may be moving along just fine, piqued and prodded excitedly, all the pieces falling into place — "it's all making sense!" — barely audible yet distinct cries bubbling forth — "yes! yeahyeahyeah, oh, yes!" — when all of a sudden the ground disappears, sense vanishes, and there before our reader sits some monstrosity, some ineffable addendum dangling just so, as if taunting the reader's hubris of thinking that he has indeed made sense of something. The "yes"s give way to a stalled "huh?" as the orgasmic frenzy of a world taking shape becomes a plaintive befuddlement.

The reader is now at a juncture. Either the sense heretofore forged needs to be adjusted or the grotesquerie needs to be incorporated, assumed, digested. The obstacle may be a mere pot hole; then again, it may demand a fundamental re-ordering of sense, of limits, a re-alignment of what the hell is going on here. A flirtatious engagement is riddled with such moments: she likes me; no, no, she finds me supremely distasteful; no, wait, she digs me, I can tell. And so on.

Reading is an extended, open event (that nevertheless operates within limits). There is no fixed or stable set of relations. A new gesture can alter the entire economy. A text may reveal itself but this revelation is never final, the emergent shape rarely stable. The revelation is perpetual (such may be the pleasure and challenge of marriage at its best: an endless discovery and reconfiguring of one's spouse and the marriage as a whole).

A reader wrestles with a text. Sometimes, things make sense, they fit; sometimes they don't. But this not-fitting is not the end of a reading. Rather, these gaps make the ensuing constellation take this or that shape. These gaps, these disjunctures, temper the rhythm of a reading.

A reader forges a path through a text according to his metabolism. He puts this here, that there. The manner in which he makes sense marks a border between his own body and the body of the text at hand. This border is as singular as the body that digests and runs through all the bodies involved. The emergent reading is the entelechy, the realization, of the possibilities that flourish between the body of the reader and the body of the text. This realization, this reading, is a productive consumption: it re-creates the world, finding new limits of both the reader and the thing.

Readers make shapes of the world. Who knows what shapes these may be? The reader must risk his sense, and his nonsense, in order to forge these exquisite constellations. And paranoia looms. Unable to find the limits of things, the proper weight, the paranoiac links radically discrepant objects together into grotesque shapes — gestures of the waiter, a snippet of conversation on the bus, a TV commercial. Unable to limit things or focus his ability to read, the paranoiac begins to substitute elaborate schemes for reading, a kind of *over-reading*. The paranoiac is the reader who fails to find the limits of things. The smallest details sprout tendrils that insinuate themselves into matters small and large, infiltrating and sullying other signs. The paranoiac reads without discretion.

Anxiety is perhaps the greatest obstacle to reading that impedes poise, inundating the senses with its own frenzy of ideas, obscuring the would-be reader's vision of the world folding, unfolding, and refolding itself. The body of the hypochondriac, that model of anxious living, is not allowed its daily machinations: the slightest twitch, an inexplicable bump, a sudden ache are signs of something else. The hypochondriac over-reads his own body, looks right over its head, as it were, to another world, a world of disease and death. Meanwhile, the life of the body goes on.

Things call out, if we know how to discern these calls. They wink, whisper, repel, they plead and beckon, they seduce. The reader not only reads things, he must discern which things to read. He must be attentive, at the ready.

Athletes provide the world with its most persistent view of the immanent reader (and an understanding of the discipline involved). A gymnast reckoning a balance beam or parallel bars must know his own weight, the weight and give of the equipment, the speed of his approach. Or a tennis player, her feet poised for whatever comes her way. Or a quarterback surveying the defense: he knows the respective speeds of the receivers and cornerbacks, he knows the strength of his own arm, the defensive line's speed, senses how long his own line can protect him. As he calls the play at the line of scrimmage — aren't we all intrigued with Peyton Manning's audibles? — the defensive line does a switch. The quarterback changes the play: rather than a slant, he calls a run up the middle.

As the batter steps to the plate, his eyes scan the field. He sees the second baseman filling the gap between second base and the first baseman: the center of the infield beckons. The pitcher throws a breaking ball; the batter chokes up, waits on the pitch, and pops the ball up the middle for a base hit. There is an infinity of such postures, an infinity of ways to be poised. Just consider the vast array of batting stances, that exquisite array of postures of readiness.

The reader is poised, equally attentive to what has happened, to what might happen, and to what is happening. And, as is the way of poise, the reader — always ready — is in a kind of repose. Poise tilts neither forwards nor backwards. And yet it is not static. Poise is the posture of the nomad, moving while always at home.

12

Diet

Diet amplifies the temporal complexities of the reading event. Eating is an odd calculus of earlier, now, later that day, and well into the future. How do you decide what to eat? How do you know what you like? How do you know what amplifies your vitality? Perhaps you've had a double espresso and brownie every day for years and they've served you well — you think keenly, write with grace, feel energized and magnified. So why not keep ordering it?

But then, one day, you have it and you find yourself with uncomfortable jitters. You can't sleep; your stomach rumbles. What's happening? Perhaps nothing; perhaps it's an aberration. Perhaps it's all good for you, fueling your health, your vitality. Or perhaps there's too much acid, too much agitation for your body as it has now become. After all, as Nietzsche says, coffee spreads darkness. In any case, diet entails a particular *now* that is always a *before* and a *later* (which, of course, is true of all immanent reading).

Sometimes, things that taste good, and even feel good, make us sick. Other times, things that taste bad, even feel bad, make us healthy — later (such as medicine). What criteria do we have to make sense of this all? Of course, there are endless medical reports — this causes colon cancer, that remedies colon cancer but causes liver damage, this helps the liver but burns a hole in the stomach. Some of this information is helpful. But often it is so abstract, so removed from the particular person and his circumstances that it is meaningless. The exemplary model doesn't suffice precisely because we are all particular. Someone can say fruit is good for you but that doesn't make it so. It depends on your body and its needs, its desires, its way of going. No, and despite the inevitable chagrin of health pundits and food columnists, there is no universal truths when it comes to diet. We are all finally alone with the menu and our stomachs.

How then does one read the intersection of body and food? It is a complex configuration of instinct and experience. Add the intellectual knowledge of medical reports and myth, and things only get more complicated. Everyone says fruit is good for the body. And yet, for some, the body recoils at the sweetness, acidity, and intensity. How does this person know whether he should eat fruit or not? We make these decisions without the certainty of proof. How can we have proof now when the proof, if there is such a thing, won't come until years later? Even then, how would we possibly know what the cause of death or disease is? The experience of the body is a billion butterfly effects.

Still, there are ways we make decisions and enjoy a kind of certainty, even if it's temporary. You learn, for instance, that if you drink too much wine, you will have a headache the next day. How much is too much? Well, that depends on the situation but is usually around four glasses. How did you come to this "usually"? From experience, of course. Then there are those times when your body declares, in no certain terms, that some food is not to be had.

And, to state the obvious, the body is not static. Just because you've always enjoyed jalapeno peppers doesn't mean you *will always* enjoy jalapeno peppers. Our bodies are constantly changing, constantly needing different things, asking for different things. Taste buds, metabolic speed, stomach acidity, bone density: it all changes, and with it what food best serves us. Making sense of diet, like making sense of all things, entails reckoning multiple moving targets as a moving target.

What constitutes "best serving" our bodies? Nietzsche says that a well-turned-out man is the one who instinctively reaches for the things that increase his vitality. In contrast, the ill-constituted man instinctively reaches for the very things that make him sick. We've all seen this: a friend or family member who insists on, say, eating fish and chips even though he knows, and everyone around him knows, that it makes him feel terrible later that night. Everyone cringes as he orders it, including his colon, but he orders it nonetheless. Cigarettes, too, bring this to life. So many smokers know that smoking is killing them — not just from reading medical reports but because now they can't walk upstairs with nearly passing out. And yet they insist on smoking, urgently and often.

This is not to say that cigarettes and fish and chips are necessarily bad for you. It's to say that each body is different and what's best for one body is not the same as what's best for another body. The criteria are not absolute. Cigarettes are not necessarily bad for you — *even if they kill you*. Causing early death does not make something necessarily bad for you. Health cannot by measured by years lived. In fact, Kierkegaard says no fate is worse than a living death — heart beating, perhaps, but being so anxious, so distracted by the inanity of this life, that you can't even die (we might call these zombies). So perhaps cigarettes make you vital, even if killing you eventually.

Our diet is a reading of our bodies in the world. There are no hard and fast, external criteria of what's healthy and what's not. All we have is this strange calculus of experience, history, knowledge, and intuition. This is no different than how we read anything: we make the most of the situation, a situation that is temporal, both forwards and backwards. We consume to drive our health and vitality and delight, all at once.

13

Will to Multiplicity

The immanent reader enjoys an odd posture that is equal parts humility and hubris — forging *a* world but not *the* world. An immanent reading does not seek to be the definitive reading. It does not want to be right. It does not want to be the only reading. On the contrary, it wants to be a reading among readings. It wants other readings just as a child wants playmates.

This is a fundamentally different will than the reader who wants to be the expert, whose book on, say, William Burroughs is supposed to be the best, the most exhaustive, with some kind of secret access to the meaning or his life or the archives. Oh, access to the archives is a golden ticket to tenure in the American university system! But while an amateur may enjoy the archives, he does not believe it makes him a good reader.

In *Poetical Dictionary*, Lohren Green critiques the traditional dictionary for not being protean. Word after word, the traditional dictionary speaks in the same voice, in the same timbre, rhythm, and style — butterfly, doodad, wheel, love, text, drool, epicurean, bolt are all written in the same voice. Why? Because the dictionary wants to be definitive, stable, a foundation: *this* is what words mean. And hence any sense of a voice, any sense that the dictionary was written by a particular person, is neutered. But of course the dictionary does have a voice — a flat, even, unmodulated voice.

This is how we imagine knowledge: it is bereft of touch, of affect. It is pure, unadulterated. Think of the science lab. It is white. The scientists wear white coats, gloves, masks. The lab is a clean zone, as if the stuff of the lab — the gloves, the white paint, the coats — were not themselves stuff with affect and mood, were not themselves constitutive of the situation, of the so-called truths. A lab is not neutral; it's white. There is no neutrality. Or, rather, neutrality is one possible reading of white. And so the traditional dictionary with its Hal-esque voice strives to be definitive through neutrality.

The immanent reader does not strive for neutrality. She does not strive to be definitive, final, absolute. This is what Green gives us with *Poetical Dictionary,* a protean standard that shifts from word to word so that bleak is, well, bleak; purple, purple; acrobat is acrobatic, even planting its landing; contraption works; gleeful is. Are these absolute definitions? No, of course not. They are readings of words that announce themselves as readings.

Poetical Dictionary not only never strives to be definitive, it actively seeks other poetical dictionaries. The traditional dictionary — which is often quite useful — declares: *No more searching, no more thinking. This is it, the final word. We're done here. Poetical Dictionary,* on the other hand, declares, *More! More readings of words! As many as we can forge! I am one among many! Bring me more!*

And what's so powerful, and so uncanny, about *Poetical Dictionary* is that it does not abandon its claim to knowledge. On the contrary, it claims to be *more* thorough — yes, a quantification of qualification — than the traditional dictionary precisely *because* it is protean, precisely because it does take the sense or mood of a word into consideration. To Green, knowledge is not predicated on certainty but on a certain mode of uncertainty:

> Rather than parsing sense from the word and uniformly imposing accuracy, clarity, concision, and simplicity, we sought to express each word's unique sense, and to do so we relied on a different, more protean standard. Of course, here too (even especially here) there is room for error. Perhaps foreplay doesn't go far enough; perhaps clumsy is too intentional, and poise leans, just slightly, forward. These are the things that keep the Editor of a *Poetical Dictionary* up at night.

There is, after all, no privileged access to the being of words, but only sometimes a happy moment in which they can be found to declare themselves a very particular (or very universal) this (Green xvi).

This is *a Poetical Dictionary,* not *the Poetical Dictionary.*

But this is not an abandonment of knowledge claims, as if poetry were ornament that came after the fact, a trope upon the foundation of literal language. Green's claim is at once supremely bold and absolutely humble. His book supersedes the traditional dictionary, tending to meaning while including the affect of the word. Affect, for Green, is knowledge that neither impedes nor adorns meaning. A word has a way of going that is simultaneously conceptual and affective.

As Green embraces affect as knowledge, knowledge becomes uncertain, unprovable: there is room for error here. *But this does not make it any less knowledge.* In fact, knowledge comes from precisely this affective participation in the world: Green discovers the sense of fetid while standing in a New York City subway. The abandonment of fixed certainty is not the abandonment of standards. On the contrary, it marks their prolif-eration. Now, there is not one standard but an infinity of standards. Odd as it sounds, the standard is protean, shifting as circumstances shift. "Rather than pairing sense from the word and uniformly imposing accuracy, clarity, concision, and simplicity, we sought to express each word's unique sense, and to do so relied on a different, more protean standard" (Green xx).

This is not to say that Green writes whatever he wants about words. No, *Poetical Dictionary* is conspicuously thorough, generous, attentive. Words enjoy pronunciation keys, clearly researched etymologies and definitions. But being thorough and being exhaustive are not the same thing. It is impossible, Green suggests, to exhaust a word. A definition is an invitation, not a reduction. There is nothing to exhaust. But there is plenty to be thorough about. He could have used words as a departing point to explore his past, his dreams, his demons, to pontificate on culture or capitalism. And all of these might have made for a certain kind of reading of the words. But Green does something else entirely. He *follows* a word wherever and however it goes — not his own memory, not his unconscious, if he even has one, but the word.

This is an idea for a book that I have long considered: a book of cosmologies. Each cosmology would make its claim that this is how the world goes — the world is all wind and earth, stillness and motion; the world is One; the world is many and never unifies; the world is made of nothing but seams; and so on. It would be a book of definitive claims about the cosmos, a book of different readings of what makes up this universe, each proffering a vision, each its own knowledge, each a universe unto itself, each a reading.

Immanent reading is baroque, enjoying a will to multiplicity.

14

Shedding Habit

There are many complex forces at work that would have us read this way or that, to have us think this way or that. The so-called news — it seems anything but — regurgitates not just the same issues but the same structure of the issues. For instance, take "the issue of abortion." Presumably, there are two sides, pro-choice and pro-life. But what if this frame is false? To even call it "abortion" is already to frame the discussion in terms of stopping something in progress. What if we were to call it a "renaissance" because it marks the rebirth of a woman's menstrual cycle? The very manner in which we think about and discuss it would change radically, shifting the focus to the woman's health and not to the would-be child. In effect, this would eliminate any need for a debate because *of course* a woman can tend to her own menstrual cycle. This is to say, the very terms in which we think are often prescribed in ways we don't even realize, by words that prefigure our thinking, and hence our reading. As Marshall McLuhan argues, environments are invisible, working at the level of habit. It is just what we do.

People often ask children: "What's your favorite color?" *As if they are supposed to have a favorite color!* But why can't kids like all colors, or multiple colors, or different colors at different times for different occasions and different reasons? The question — seemingly innocent — carries with it an entire ideology, a paradigm of assumptions that privileges the singular, the hierarchy, and the absolute. To shed habit, we must be rigorous about exploding such innocent assumptions. To shed habit, we must question the question.

Take how we talk about movies. People say, "That character was not believable," or "the plot was silly," or "the story didn't hold together." Many times, all these things might be true. But identification and plot consistency are tactics of reading, tactics amongst tactics. And they are ones that strive for sameness: how is that character like me (or like someone I know)? How does it all cohere?

But there are other ways to view films. I taught a film class once entitled "Bring on the Strange." We watched a series of films and worked actively not to view them as good or bad — that egregious, insidious thumbs-up/thumbs-down — but to engage these films in their difference, in their oddity. We looked at how they assembled themselves, how they assembled the world, how they situated us as viewers. We read for the difference the film proffered, not the sameness.

Narrative is one possibility of film but is by no means necessary. In fact, plot comes from the written word and its movement from left to right. Film, on the other hand, enjoys a fundamental non-linearity — especially as we employ the digital which has no reason to be wound on a reel. Film offers simultaneity, an allatonceness that novels find difficult. (William Burroughs, inspired by film, pushed writing towards simultaneity with cuts-ups, fold-ins, and rearrangements of the page.) Consider any scene in a film. Look at all those details, all the things your eye may pass over because they look familiar — the trees, the cars, the wrinkles, the twitches, the sky, the garbage, the knick-knacks. Most Hollywood filmmakers do their best to control all these details so everything in view refers to some common theme — the camera zooms over the Cure poster on the wall, the black clothes on the floor, the headphones next to the bed and we know this is a cool, smart, but troubled teen. Clichés abound. Hollywood deploys the cliché to confirm the viewers' sense of life, to confirm the prescribed order of things. Nothing new happens.

But none of these things — all the things a camera captures — needs to add up to anything other than what we see on the screen. All those details need not refer. They can just insist, persist, when and where they are, allatonce. Look at how Wong Kar Wai relishes the details of the quotidian, details that don't signify anything but that nonetheless — and perhaps *therefore* — enthrall, entice, delight. When taken together, none of this stuff — the clock on the wall, the clothes, the wallpaper — adds up to anything other than the experience of that scene, if scene is even the right word.

Why a scene, anyway? What is a scene? Do films need scenes? Do they need characters? Do they need dialog? Do they need the words spoken to make sense? Do films need one screen? Why not one screen filled with multiple screens? We've seen some mainstream experimentation with this — *The Thomas Crown Affair, Time Code, Woodstock, Buffalo '66*. But why not assume from the get go that the screen is in fact multiple, a screen of screens?

In order to read the world — to view films, read books, taste our food — we need to shed the habits that blind us. We need to question the question. Just because someone asks something — "Did you like the film?" — doesn't mean you have to answer it. You can ask a different question altogether or answer something else entirely. Questions are insidious as they initiate a local social contract; they seemingly obligate the listener. But to read, one must be willing to break this contract and write a new one, one in which the frame is open rather than predefined.

We need to break the clichés that lure us into the same, into the familiar. To read a thing means being alive to how that thing distributes the world, to the science it offers, to the pedagogy it proffers. To go well with things one must tend to those things, not regurgitate the inherited.

Shedding habit demands great attention, fortitude, and, alas, alienation from the social. Don't be surprised if people don't enjoy talking to you — or, more likely, you don't enjoy talking to people — about politics, films, books, ideas. Thanks to a ubiquitous media that is shockingly coherent in its framing of various discussions — I'll never cease to be amazed that, of all the possible things to report, newspapers and TV news all report on the same things — people fall into the same habits of thought. They assume you're either a conservative or liberal (or perhaps some extreme they don't want to consider so they dismiss you as some kind of nut; indeed, this is one of the tactics of the habitual world: to define anything outside its scope as insane). In some areas, religion is a good in and of itself; in others, it's a bad in and of itself. But what if your opinions are complex, not just ambivalent but multivalent? Perhaps it's not a question of whether you "believe in god" or not. Perhaps it's a matter of *how* you believe what you believe. In any case, once you question the question, you may find yourself gloriously alone.

Still, how does one go about shedding habit, asking different questions? Derangement of both senses and cognition can be effective. This can be achieved through different practices — music, art, drugs, sex, physical exertion, extended silence, sustained noise. We fall into patterns, hearing, seeing, smelling, tasting, thinking the same things. Contemporary life — and perhaps all human life, if not all life — tends towards repetition of the same. The school day, work day, television programming, open and closing of stores: they all work in conjunction forming a network of familiar triggers and behaviors. This informs how we read the world, often blinding us with the sheer pervasiveness of the familiar. Breaking these patterns — introducing new ones by literally scrambling the patterns of perceptions — can wake us up to the way of things.

Go on a color walk: choose a color — blue — and go where you see blue. See nothing but blue. Turn your day blue. See the infinite variations of blue. Go with blue and let blue pervade your blood.

Terence McKenna recommends smoking DMT. Three big puffs of this spirit molecule and you're transported into other dimensions. In his words, you will be *astonished* — not just amazed but astonished:

> Under the influence of DMT, the world becomes an Arabian labyrinth, a palace, a more than possible Martian jewel, vast with motifs that flood the gaping mind with complex and wordless awe. Color and the sense of a reality-unlocking secret nearby pervade the experience. There is a sense of other times, and of one's own infancy, and of wonder, wonder and more wonder. It is an audience with the alien nuncio. (http://www.seren dipity.li/dmt/chris_v.html)

Everything you know, everything you take for granted, everything you assume life to be will be altered — for five to seven minutes:

> We can all smoke DMT, or you can make it your business to now find out about this, and see for yourself. And not everybody agrees with me. I mean, some people say it wasn't anything like that. But some people agree, and I think if you get two out of ten agreeing with a rap like this, then you'd better pay attention. (http://deoxy.org/h_twhat.htm)

There's that excellent scene in *I Heart Huckabees* in which Jason Schwartzman and Mark Wahlberg discover a temporary answer to breaking the monotony, and pain, of the quotidian: they hit each other in the face with a big red ball. In *Fight Club*, men pound each other, maul each other, to escape the soul-numbing drone of the everyday.

Of course, sensory and cognitive derangement can be as equally blinding and obscuring as any habit — and, of course, such deranging can itself become a habit. Don Juan tells Carlos Castaneda that drugs were necessary *for him*, Carlos, to experience the magic universe, not necessary in general. It all depends on the circumstances, on what this or that system demands.

In *Francis Bacon: The Logic of Sense*, Deleuze argues that the painter does not stand before an empty canvas and figure out what to paint. He stands before a dense canvas, a canvas filled to the brim with received images, with clichés. The artist's job, then, is to cut away, destroy, carve this density of images in order to make something new. Francis Bacon would begin by marring the canvas, taking a broom with paint and making seemingly random marks on the canvas. And, based on these, he'd construct his images.

And yet this, too, can become cliché, does become cliché. Consider what happened to Pollock's drips or to Warhol's multihued silkscreens — they became tropes of image software.

In any case, in order to read the way of things, we have to work to shed habit. This does not mean we have to make ourselves empty. There is no pure now, no pure event, as if there were a reality that flourished just below the surface of this world. To read the way of things well does not mean evacuating yourself. It means making perception an event that emerges between and amongst readers, things, concepts, knowledge, histories, desires, perceptions, moods. The beginner's mind, in this case, is not blank. On the contrary, it is full yet open. It is a consuming, engaging plenum. To shed habit is not to empty oneself but to become oneself.

15

A Thing among Things

An immanent reader is not the stability amidst the flux, the anchor in the storm. She is a thing among things, in flux along with the rest of it. It's all so much stuff happening.

In *Matter and Memory*, Henri Bergson claims that everything is an image. That is to say, everything is something that is perceived. This includes our bodies, our nerves, our brains. The brain is not something that is distinct from the world. It is made of the same stuff of the world. It is stuff just as a piece of paper, a flower, a mug are stuff. Ideas, too — and notions, thoughts, dreams, concepts: they are stuff, as well, even if invisible. This different stuff enjoys different properties, different ways of going, but they are not, in Bergson's words, different in kind but in degree of complexity.

Things go with other things in myriad ways — ricocheting, marbling, repelling, conjoining, synergizing. Just as different things interact with pavement differently — a glass shatters, a ball bounces, a head fractures — a reader and a thing can go together any number of ways.

This is not to say that a human being (can we say a human becoming?) just sits there inert, a thing in the worst sense of the word. No, a reader is a productive cog in the circuit of life, a productive node in the ever-emergent network of the cosmos. The reader may not be a master or an expert who is removed from the world. But the reader is an amateur at play in the world, Hunter Thompson spending a year riding with the Angels only to get stomped. The reader gets dirty. The reader *is* dirty, in the best sense of the word. The reader's knowledge does not come from objectivity, from standing back from the fray. On the contrary, it comes from being in the midst of it all. As Merleau-

Ponty says, we only see because we are something that can be seen. We are *of* the flesh of the world, at once constituent and constitutive.

The German artist Jochem Hendricks created an artist's reading machine. As his eyes traverse this or that, as they look the thing over, the movements are recorded. For instance, he reads the newspaper. The machine tracks his eye movement in the process. Meanwhile, on a blank newspaper nearby, these movements are captured. The new newspaper is a repetition of the other one, the one with words and images, the one delivered to your home. This new one is singular, born of the engagement between Hendricks' eyes, the process of reading, and the paper. You can see how his eyes traveled along the maze that is the contemporary newspaper, when his eyes lingered over an image, when they moved to a new column.

In some sense, it is a parody of reading. Hendricks gives us a clear model of productive consumption as the very act of consuming the newspaper produces the art. Indeed, the title of his piece is *Lesen* — German for "reading" or "to read." The reader is a productive cog within the circuit of consumption and production. The reader is not a master, forging the world from raw clay. Rather, Hendricks comes to a world already in progress — the material is literally always already read, a newspaper — and offers himself as a node in the network. So much stuff, yes, but an inflection point within the flow of stuff.

But it would be a mistake, as well, to think that of reading as mediation. Merleau-Ponty's claims that, for Cézanne, reading is in fact immediate. To read is to participate in a thing as it makes itself for the very first time; it is an event of which both the reader and the object are constituents. Cézanne and pear interact in such a way — like skull and pavement, wind and leaves, land and river — to make that painting there. It would equally be a mistake to think that Pollock does not read as he writhes over the canvas. After all, each drip navigates the circuit of viscosity — the viscosity of paint and of desire: this drip should be brown and go approximately there, this one white and dripping its drip here, and so on, even if chance plays its role as well. Pollock reads his own paintings as they emerge, a cog within the engine of his "own" paintings. A Pollock painting *is* a circuit that includes, but is not determined by, Pollock's body, Pollock's style, paint, and canvas.

Reading is not a matter of a human who stands apart from things, taking in the world and putting everything in its proper conceptual place, in its proper categorical buckets. The reader is a thing; the thing is a thing. To read is an encounter between two things. Just as wind rustles leaves and leaves, in turn, inflect the wind; just as concrete and a glass vase enjoy a tense relationship; just as light and lens interact just so to make images; just as coffee makes my body and thinking faster; so the reader and the thing go together as they do and will.

The reader, generously, lends the world his body. And the world, in kind, returns the favor. It's all stuff going with stuff.

16

The Middle Voice, or Subjective vs. Perspective, with Constant Reference to Merleau-Ponty

Picture Jochem Hendricks reading the newspaper and, in the process, making a new newspaper. Is he active? Or passive? Or do those categories no longer apply? As a thing among things, and not the master of the encounter, the immanent reader speaks in a different register. To read immanently is to speak in a voice that is neither active nor passive, that is both active and passive. It is to operate in a middle voice.

Picture a house. This house can be approached from different angles and perspectives. This multiplicity of perspectives never disappears; we never see the whole house. Nor is there a house that is *not* seen. So in what sense can we say there is a house? "The house itself is not the house seen from nowhere, but the house seen from everywhere. The completed object is translucent, being shot through from all sides by an infinite number of present scrutinies which intersect in its depths leaving nothing hidden" (M-P, PP 69). The house is "not one *in spite of* the changes of perspective, but *in* that change or *through* it" (90). This house is bound by an odd, ideal, and yet thoroughly worldly limit: a near-infinity of simultaneous perspectives.

And yet when I approach a house, I never see it from all those perspectives. That would be absurd. No, *I* see the object from *here and now*: "But, once more, my human gaze never *posits* more than one facet of the object, even though by means of horizons it is directed towards the others" (69). There is a thing. And this thing is neither completely subjective, an internal conjuring, nor is it "for itself," as if it were independent of this world. The house is "for us" (71). And yet this "for us" does not capture the object in its entirety; this moment does not and cannot substitute for the whole (what in rhetoric is called *synecdoche*). Rather, the perspective is one moment of the object, continuous *with* the whole but not speaking *for* the whole (metonymy). As an incarnate subject in an incarnate world, I interact with this thing here. I meet it and it meets me, and together we make the world.

This is my perspective, my view — visual, yes, but also affective, cognitive, sensual — of a thing. I am not a removed bystander exempt from the pull of objects, the fray of interaction. "If the status of the object is profoundly changed, so also is that of the subject" (Deleuze, FLB 19). The reader shifts along with the text, the thing. The four-ball changes as it is hit, just as the cue ball changes, just as the table as a whole changes, just as the positions within the game change. Like the pool table, perception is an emergent system made up of multiple factors — things, readers, memories, smells, digestive health. My perspective on the house is not the product of my *subjective* sensibilities, as if I were a stable quantity reacting to the world about me. I am figured *in*, and *with*, the variability of the house. I come to a view of it just as it comes to my view.

Consider seeing. Is seeing active or passive? Do you see the coffee mug? Or does the coffee mug, in a sense, project itself into you — into your head, into your body, the very vision of it filling you just as the coffee itself does as you drink it? Do you come to the world? Or does the world come to you? Or is this a false dichotomy? Is it that we come together, we become together, we are both stuffs of this world and we go and interact as any stuffs in the world go — colliding, harmonizing, snuggling? Vision — all perception — is neither active nor passive, is both active and passive.

The place of perspective, of reading, is the middle, between here and there, between you and me. It happens in what we call the middle voice. The middle voice is difficult to speak, at least in English. English has subjects of sentences that stand separate from their actions, the verbs, which in turn act upon subjects. "I kiss you": in this simple construction there is a distinct I, a distinct kiss, and a distinct you. There is an implied, and obligatory, distinction between who I am and the actions I take, as if there were a me that stands apart from the world, that comes before, or outside, action, as if there were a kiss that did not involve me and you. In some sense, all there is is this kissing — there is no I, no kiss, no you, just this cooperative event (hopefully!) of me, kiss, desire, you.

In *On the Genealogy of Morals*, Nietzsche writes that when we say "lightning strikes," we are being redundant. Of course lightning strikes. What is lightning if it doesn't strike? Lightning is that which strikes; it is striking, always and already. Take away the striking and you have nothing. When we say "lightning strikes," we put a doer behind the deed when, for Nietzsche, all there is is the deed (45). Nietzsche argues that one of the great moves made by the slaves was to posit a subject behind the action who could be held eternally responsible for his actions — the bird of prey becomes guilty of eating the little lamb, as if the bird had a choice, as if the bird were not always and already a bird that preys. The invention of this doer is the invention of Judeo-Christian morality and its arsenal of ego, morality, guilt, and judgment.

Our grammar rests on such a subject who is distinct from both his actions and the world. And so here we posit a middle voice, a way to speak that is neither active nor passive. In English, this demands that we make language perform in such a way that the distinctions between doer, deed, and object are intertwined. We have to make language enmesh and touch and palpate.

When we speak in the middle voice, we speak a certain intimacy between subject and object. In the words of Merleau-Ponty, seer and seen are chiasmatically intertwined as "the seer and the visible reciprocate one another and we no longer know which sees and which is seen" (VI 135). And this, Merleau-Ponty argues, is the very foundation of experience and knowledge. That is to say, our intertwining with the world is not an obstacle to knowing the world; it is rather the very way we know the world: "the thickness of the flesh between the seer and the thing is constitutive for the thing of its visibility as for the seer of his corporeity; it is not an obstacle between them, it is their means of communication" (ibid). I can only know the world *precisely because I am so much stuff, precisely because the world and I are continuous.* The so-called epistemological problems of philosophers — how can we come to know the world? — are false problems with false questions. Here, we are suggesting that there is no ontological gap between the world and me that creates an epistemological impossibility. On the contrary, the stuff of the world and the stuff of me are more-or-less the same (while being relentlessly differentiated).

To know is not to stand at a remove and categorize into concepts. Knowing is part and parcel of an interaction, an encounter with things. I take up a tree and all kinds of things happen — I smell the wood, feel the grain, sneeze at the allergens, hide from my friends, recognize this as an oak. All sorts of things happen between tree and me. We may say all of them are knowing or we may say only the conceptual categorization is knowing. It depends on our reading of "to know." But in any case this knowing is constitutive *and* constituent of the encounter.

A relationship emerges between the tree and me, between what was once subject and once object (we are trying to move away from this dichotomy). This relationship is fundamentally relative and yet this relativity does not stand in relation to a fixed center, norm, or essence. This relation is a certain perspective on and within the variable declension of the object. There is a singularity of this occasional place — tree and me — which is self-organizing and self-sustaining while nonetheless partaking of all the generalities of tree and me. It does not need permission and it is not determined from afar by a concept; the concepts and ideas are constitutive of the encounter. The tree and I work it out together, even as this together involves memories, concepts, knowledge, grass, bushes, bugs, splinters, categories.

Reading happens in the middle voice. The interaction of reader and text is an intertwining and fundamentally co-operative event, even if said event is hostile or violent. As I read or listen, "I am receiving and giving in the same gesture" (M-P, PW 11). I give my knowledge, my experience, of language and of the world to a thing and it returns the favor.

This is not a re-union; this is not a going-home. The reader must go where he has not been. "In other words: to look at an object is to inhabit it, and from this habitation to grasp all things in terms of the aspects which they present to it" (M-P, PP 68). It is an alien possession in which reader, via his engagement, comes to see the world, grasp the world, anew. In reading, both thing and reader are reconstituted, led astray of themselves.

Reading is not a matter of "understanding" per se. It is not a conceptual categorization. To perceive an object is not a matter of reading its signs, of understanding its code. To perceive an object is to engage with it, to touch it, physically, conceptually. We do not read or interpret or understand *signs*; we engage *aspects* of the thing.

To read is a matter of engaging, experiencing, of dwelling: it is a matter of mutual appropriation. And this appropriation moves in both directions; I grasp the text as it grasps me: "When I am listening, it is not necessary that I have an auditory perception of the articulated sounds but that the conversation pronounces itself within me. It summons me and grips me; it envelops and inhabits me to the point where I cannot tell what comes from me and what from it" (M-P, PW 19).

I engage a text as it engages me, with my entire distributive scheme, my configuring, of possible bodies: words, breath, time, concepts, affect. With my body, I follow the style of the text before me — a book, a chair, Hegel, a smile. But this is not *subjective*. It is *perspectival*. "Subject" sets me apart from the world, isolates me in my private manias, private experience. And while I do certainly enjoy such private, subjective experiences this is not what we are talking about here. To read is to announce one's perspective, one's way of participating in, through, and with things. Subjective is internal; perspective is external, one's view on things.

Reading is a deed, an event. Reading is lightning always already striking. Reading yields what Deleuze and Guattari call a bloc of becoming as thing and reader mutually inflect each other. When a reader reads, he makes the world. And, in turn, is made.

17

The Uncanny Time of Reading

Reading does not happen after a thing. There is not first a thing and then the reading. A thing is always already read, always already inscribed with glances, touch, thoughts, categories, knowledge, history. There is no pure this, no pure that. There are only things that go.

A thing *is* all of its possible readings (exemplary, immanent, or otherwise).

This is not to say that a thing only exists via human eyes, human experience. On the contrary, it is to say that human eyes, human senses, are always already touching. All things — humans, animals, arts, rocks, notions — are always already participating in the world, always already networked, always already networks themselves. A thing is always already making sense.

This sense changes with time, with circumstance. A horse in a field pulling a plow is not a horse on a racetrack and neither is a horse walking beneath a cop through Manhattan traffic. In some sense, those are three different animals that form their own networks: the field horse may be akin to an ox or tractor; a racehorse, to NASCAR; a police horse, to a motorcycle. Of course, from another perspective — namely, that of a zoologist — it is one animal: a horse (or perhaps *Equus ferus caballus*).

When my son was young, I was showing him a picture book when we came upon the image of a zebra. He said, quite sensibly, "Mooo."

A good reading reveals possibilities — after my son's reading, zebras and cows are forever intertwined along the network of black and white. A good reading extends a thing, opens the network, forges new connections between things.

This extension is also a production. The reading is latent in the thing, perhaps. But the reading emerges from an encounter of a thing with other things — including with the reader (which may be a car, a wall, squirrel, or person). So when does a reading happen? Is it already there? Does it happen in the very act of reading? I'd say the answer is both: a reading is at once latent and produced. One might say that the production produces the latency after the fact. Reading is uncanny. It takes the familiar and makes it unfamiliar. And vice versa.

To read something, and to read it well, is fundamentally to change that thing — and hence to change the world. Reading inflects and shapes the very fabric of existence. A good reading moves the world in an exciting, delightful, thrilling fashion taking us all along for the ride.

And it leads to new possibilities of thinking, new possibilities of perceiving, new possibilities of living. It does not proffer the purely alien (if that's even possible). No, a good reading *repeats* this world: it takes it up from within a life in progress and forges a new life. It does not *copy* the world; it does not *imitate* the world. A good reading *repeats*.

Repetition is a strange figure. To repeat is to differentiate the world, take it up and distribute it in a novel way. Such a reading — one that repeats rather than copies or reduces — reconstitutes the known and the already and in so doing must necessarily speak the language of the known and the already — only in a new timbre, rhythm, and perhaps meaning something else entirely. And so it seems as if, perhaps, we already know this thing. But then again we do not. It is at once familiar and unfamiliar: it is uncanny.

Repetition is in fact the very condition of language. All words already exist. Grammar, for the most part, already exists. And yet we are able to take these things that already exist and use them in new ways. Isn't this the stuff of great writing? Nabokov uses the same words as Melville as Dickens as Emerson and you and I. And yet each somehow, miraculously, manages to make something new of it, something new of these words — new experiences, new combinations, new possibilities, new ways of going. These writers take things we know so well — words! — and make them undulate, pulsate, radiate, and resonate. They make them familiar and unfamiliar at the same time.

Clearly, what Nabokov and Melville and Emerson do is not just *copy* existing language. We know what it looks like when someone copies — it rings "false." To copy something is to cop the most outward tropes of a thing. But to repeat a thing is to inhabit it from the inside out, to crawl into its skin and then start moving about. Repetition is nothing less than a miracle whereby the known becomes known again as if for the very first time: it is the relentlessly uncanny movement from the familiar to the unfamiliar and back.

And yet the uncanny is itself uncanny, bearing a very strange relationship to the past and a very strange temporal configuration in general. The uncanny, while moving from the familiar to the unfamiliar, or rather occupying the space of the familiar and the unfamiliar at the same time, is not a derivative of the known. There is not first the familiar and then the unfamiliar. In fact, a good reading reverses the relationship and makes the unfamiliar familiar and the familiar unfamiliar. It's not, as Hamlet suggests, that time is out of joint. It's that time is multi-jointed.

This is all to say that the movement from the familiar to the unfamiliar and back is not a linear progression but a perpetual state of flux in which the world is at once known and not known at the same time.

Immanent reading operates in precisely this space. There is no standard from which to deviate; there is just going, this way and that. Everything is an uncertainty and glorious for it. Reading is the art of participating in the moving world while one is moving oneself. The world is always itself and always changing. In the words of Brion Gysin, "Who runs may read but few people run fast enough. What are we here for? Does the great metaphysical nut revolve around that? Well, I'll crack it for you, right now. What are we here for? We are here to go!"

The temporality of reading is not the old linear trajectory of author > book > reader. Put aside the architecture that would proffer a foundation first on which the edifice rests. Put aside, at least for a moment, the will to a foundation, to an origin, to an absolute beginning. A reading is not a deviation of the known. The world is uncanny from the get-go.

Consider the cover song. Presumably, The Rolling Stones wrote "Satisfaction." OK, maybe. But which version is the original one? The one, probably not recorded, of Mick Jagger strumming on a guitar and humming it for Keith Richards? The one with Brian Jones playing harmonica? Is it the version they did live at this or that club? The 1965 mono single? Or the stereo re-release in the '80s? The song is always a repetition of itself: look for the original and you find a series.

Now add Devo's astounding version to the mix. I'd argue that when Devo covers "Satisfaction," it became the original: just as Mick and Keith are constantly repeating the song, extending it, reaching for its limit, so does Devo — and Devo finds things that Mick and Keith never could have. Some might say Cat Power's is the real one; others might claim Brittney or Bjork with PJ Harvey. Each seeks to repeat a song that was always already a repetition of itself.

There is no original version. There's nothing but versions — versions to infinity.

18

Words

But don't words refer to meanings? Aren't they symbols that stand in for ideas and things? Don't they get their value, their power, their meaning from reality as well as from ideas?

Well, that's one reading of language and one technology of the word. In a referential reading of language, words are arbitrary. They are sensual markers that refer or point to things or ideas. Take the word dog, for instance. "Dog" is a sound, and a visual mark — a glyph — that in and of itself is gibberish. But it points to what really matters, to what we imagine is the real thing: that dog there, or the idea of dogs in general (which is already confusing: where does "dog" point?). In this mechanics, the physical gives way to the metaphysical; the body gives way to a soul; the word gives way to meaning.

This is the model of language for exemplary readers. Someone who reads things as examples of something else sees this thing here — this word, this text — as giving way to something more stable, something certain, to a category of knowledge, just as a word gives way to its real meaning, to an idea or real thing.

Immanent reading operates with a different model of language and of the word, one in which the physical and metaphysical, word and meaning, are intimately intertwined. Neither is primary. The mark does not determine the meaning and the meaning does not determine the mark. They inflect each other. They go together in a complex and ever-differing calculus of relations.

Word and thing do not refer to each other. They forge a network. Let's take dog again. There's my neighbor's dog, Lucky; Lucky's predecessor, Tiny; the word, "dog"; the word for dog in French, "chien"; the well-known sexual position, doggy style; a photograph of Lucky; a painterly portrait of Tiny; the idea of a dog; my little boy pretending to be a dog; and so on. None of these are the *real* dog. They are *repetitions* of dog, each one defining dog in its own way, from its own perspective — but still somehow remaining dog. They form a network, a collage, a dog conspiracy, if you will. There's no idea of dog that hovers above them all — because even that idea is a repetition, is part of the network.

This is the very premise of Lohren Green's distinctive *Poetical Dictionary* in which he defines words according to their particular logic and way of going. So rather than one voice defining all words in the same manner, the only difference being content, Green defines words in the manner best befitting that word — glee is gleeful, bleak is bleak, purple is purple, acrobatic plants its landing, and so on. A word, for Green, is a way of going that is simultaneously conceptual, sensual, and affective. When he defines a word, he takes all of these things into consideration — unlike the traditional dictionary for which glee is serious, butterfly is serious, silly is serious. The traditional dictionary imagines that we can separate a word from its meaning by using the same deadpan voice to speak all words. It imagines that we can isolate the concept from the brute physicality of the word, a Judeo-Christian-Platonist inheritance.

But what Green gives us is a whole other order of things in which flesh and soul, mark and idea, are necessarily and intimately intertwined. Maurice Merleau-Ponty uses the trope of the chiasm to speak of this intertwining, this marbling.

I think this is important so I'll spend some time trying to explain what I'm talking about. Or, rather, how I read Merleau-Ponty talking about such things.

Language, says Merleau-Ponty, is essentially physiognomic: "We have this acquisition [of language] as we have arms and legs" (Signs 19). In fact, "there is not a word, not a form of behavior which does not owe something to purely biological being" (M-P, PP 189). Words are particular and possible forms of bodily behavior, "one of the possible uses of my body. I reach back for the word as my hand reaches towards the part of my body which is being pricked" (180).

This fleshy language is not a system of signs that *designates* meaning. Language does not represent. In fact, there really is no such thing as language. Where could it possibly be? How could we ever look at it, study it, examine it? Language runs all the way through us — our thoughts, bodies, blood, memories, dreams, concepts. Just as seer and seen are intertwined, words and world are intertwined, language and bodies are intertwined. We can't sift out our flesh in order to discover words in their purity. There is no language per se. There are only actions, events, deeds that go in the shape and way of glee, purple, bleak, this.

The basic unit of meaning is not the sign. It is the gesture: *"language never says anything; it invents a series of gestures"* (M-P, PW 32). "The spoken word is a genuine gesture, and it contains its meaning in the same way as the gesture contains it. This is what makes communication possible... The spoken word is a gesture, and its meaning, a world" (M-P, PP 183). This gesture is not itself a sign but is an aspect: "The gesture *does not make me think* of anger, it is anger itself" (184). The gesture does not point to or designate something that is over there — a thought or thing or event. The gesture is a distribution of the physical and the meta-physical, of bodies, breath, notions, concepts, ideas.

This gesture does not stand in for the whole of the event but is one of a series of intermingling spatio-temporal components. There is no longer any question of the relationship between signifier and signified, no Lacanian algebra. "[T]he central phenomenon of language," writes Merleau-Ponty, "is in fact *the common act of the signifying and the signified*" (Signs 95).

Meaning is not to be found outside the text, outside the words. We do not have recourse to a code or a system into which we can plug our utterances in order to decode them and discover their meaning. But before hearing this familiar Derridean call, neither does meaning fail as it is perpetually deferred. For Merleau-Ponty, meaning is immanent to the word *qua* gesture. The gesture is not reducible to anything outside itself; it is not a *deviation* from a proper or normal meaning; nor is it a *derivation* of a previously established system. It is the *inauguration* of meaning: "[I]t is the birth of a norm and is not realized according to a norm; it is the identity of the external and the internal and not the projection of the internal in the external" (M-P, PP 61). This gesture is self-organizing, self-sustaining, autopoetic: "The linguistic gesture, like all the rest, delineates its own meaning" (186). When we read a text, we confront a novel language. It is our task as reader to learn this new language rather than assume language has failed or apply the rules we've learned elsewhere.

Meaning is forged on the go. Behavior, not conceptual designation or reference, creates meaning. *Meaning is the very activity of the body as it moves through the world,* arms doing this, legs that, the stomach rumbling just so, words uttered in just such a pitch, in just such a rhythm, inflecting sense and meaning and mood. Each utterance is a linguistic gesture that constitutes a way of operating in the world, of distributing the world, which is perhaps to say the same thing. The linguistic gesture, as with all gestures, "is the manner itself in which we meet the situation and live it" (189). Language is an affirmative activity of the body that configures the world as it goes:

> What then does language express, if it does not express thoughts? It presents or rather it *is* the subject's taking up a position in the world of his meanings... The phonetic 'gesture' brings about, both for the speaking subject and for his hearers, a certain modulation of existence, exactly as a pattern of my bodily behavior endows the objects around me with a certain significance both for me and for others. (193)

Meaning is generated in, through, and by the body of the utterer, by and in what *this* body does in, to, of, and with the world.

Paul Ricoeur argues that the word alone cannot be a site of meaning; it is the trope as a relationship between words that creates meaning. The structuralists offer a variant of this same argument: a word only has meaning in its difference from other words, its value defined by its relation within an economic exchange of all words within a language. For Merleau-Ponty, however, a word is already a "coherent deformation," is already a gesture, is always and already a stylized moment of the world. A word always and already bears meaning, is always a particular manner of assembling the world. "Voluptuous" is, well, voluptuous; "arcane" twists elusively away from our grasp; "ingratiate" insinuates itself with an almost slippery backhand-edness.

A word is already a reading. Take the word "moon." Now consider it in French, "la lune." These are two very different readings of that big thing that sometimes shines and sometimes doesn't, that floats or hangs or moves through our sky. Moon, presumably, comes from a root meaning measure, as in measuring time through the phases of that big sky-rock; ergo, the word month. *La lune*, however, speaks to the light of that big sky-rock. Neither is right; neither is wrong. They are spins, takes, readings. They each amplify a different aspect of the thing.

In a sense, a word is a perception of things, an inflected manner of appropriation. It wraps its tendrils around things, events, concepts — and of course vice-versa: the world insemi-nates the word, a chiasmus of the visible and invisible. The result is the word *qua* gesture, an entire configuring of things; the word enjoys a posture in the world that always bares an intimate relationship with the world.

In Nietzsche's early lectures on rhetoric, we encounter much the same argument. He declares in one early lecture, "There is obviously no unrhetorical 'naturalness' of language to which one could appeal; language itself is the result of purely rhetorical arts" (21). The word does not grasp the essence of a thing; it does not stand in for this or that thing; nor does it designate this or that thing. Rather, it marks a relationship between me and the thing: "It is not the things that pass over into consciousness, but the manner in which we stand toward them." And this relationship is marked not by words or signs per se but by tropes: "all words are tropes in themselves, and from the beginning" (23).

Language happens now. But things are not so simple. Merleau-Ponty writes that "it is the very notion of the immediate which is transformed: henceforth the immediate is no longer the impression, the object which is one with the subject, but the meaning, the structure, the spontaneous arrangement of parts" (58). What emerges is the strange temporal activity of *repetition*: "In the living exercise of speech there is really a repetition of all preceding experience, an appeal to the fulfillment of language, a presumptive eternity" (M-P, PW 41–42).

Repetition is a creative gesture inaugurated by the operator of language; repetition is a matter of living-through. That is, where recollection is a cognitive function, a looking-backwards, a kind of non-living precisely because the event has to have already happened, repetition happens from the inside: "the interiority of movement, is *not opposition, not mediation,* but repetition" (Deleuze, DR 10). The operator of language is a repeater. "Thus there is indeed an interior of language, a signifying intention which animates linguistic events and at each moment, makes language a system capable of its own self-recovery and self-confirmation," of its own repetition (M-P, PW 36). To engage in language is to create from the inside of language, to move outwards from the middle; language happens from the perspective of the user within the event rather than from a virtual system or code or as instances of the double law of *différance.* For Merleau-Ponty, words are always and already gestures which are created, repeated, by an uttering subject as a way of handling the world, distributing the world, as a way of living.

19

Images

But what about images (at least visual images; everything, says Bergson, is an image)? How are we to make sense of them, to read them?

Just as we read words: as events that take up and distribute the world. An image is not an image *of* — although, sometimes, it is *also* an image of. A camera doesn't take pictures of things. It grabs information, not forms. It takes in light, not objects. As for painting, those are just marks. Forms emerge from the conspiracy of marks just as forms always emerge in this world (at the same time that they dissolve).

An image, like a word, is a way of going, of taking up the world — a face, a sunset, light, sadness, love, ambivalence, things — and assembling them just so. Like a word, an image selects, inflects, arranges, and prioritizes. This is not to say that an image is not intimately enmeshed with the thing in the picture. Of course it is. A picture of me is a picture of me. But it is not *solely* a picture of me. It is another me, another thing in the world, another way of going. The image of me is simultaneously a reading of me and its own thing.

An image is not a re-presentation. It is a repetition. An image of me is me again and anew. Neither the image of me nor this me is the real one. Or, rather, we are both real but in different ways. Obviously, an image of me is not covered under the same legal jurisdiction that I am: tear the picture of me in two and you will not be arrested for assault (but you may for damage to property). An image circulates in its own network of economies — legal, financial, interpretive. This network intersects the network that is me. Together, we inflect each other more or less depending on the node within the network, the junctures of the diverse economies.

In any case, I am suggesting than an image is not a derivation or a supplement of the real. In the logic of repetition, there is no original, no master term: we are always already supplemental. Or, to put it more affirmatively, everything is a point of origin, everything is the center of its world — just as it is a periphery in another word. All the terms are repetitions that inflect each other. Isn't this the way of fame — that the relentless image-making of a person changes that person?

An image, like any thing, is a multiplicity, a more-or-less elaborate network of affects, effects, speeds, intensities. It is a metabolic engine. A camera doesn't as much capture the world as it does digest it and reassemble it. An image-maker, then, does not make a picture *of* the world. He *proliferates* the world, making more and more of it.

And so we return to our initial question: how are we to read images? Well, just as we do things and words. We go with them. This means that rather than seeking to *identify* an image, or even identify *with* an image, we open ourselves to being moved by and with the image. Rather than saying, "Hey, I know what that is! That's me!" we declare, "I *don't* know what that is! I wonder how it can take me up, distribute me, move me in ways I didn't know possible!"

Take an exhibit of photographic portraits by Richard Avedon. Here is room after room filled with face after face. And there is your face coming face to face with face after face. Each face inflects the world just so, in impossibly subtle ways, as only a face really can. Oh, the face is extraordinary in that it is at once screen and camera, taking in the world and playing it back, all the while making sense through an elaborate and particular algorithm that is a body, a memory, and taste. As your face takes in the infinite differences of each face, it becomes another face in this hall of faces — a face playing back all these faces in its own fashion. Face-to-face with all these faces, the face of the viewer becomes a face amongst faces, another image.

Henri Bergson says everything is an image — blood, nerves, brain, body, flowers, things. What he means by this is that everything exists in and through our perception of it, whether that thing is a photograph, a body, a film. After all, what is a thing if it is not, finally, as we perceive it? Bergson's claim is that this is not some convoluted philosophic claim. On the contrary, it is quite practical: that thing there is just as I perceive it. My senses don't mislead me or fail me. I have no reason to distrust them. The world is as it happens to me.

This is not to say that there is a perception that is naïve, pure, a way of perceiving things in themselves. My perception is necessarily wound up with my memory, my metabolism, my body. My perception of the world is a palpable event that quite literally moves me this way or that. I am image; that is image. We confront each other, move each other, inflect each other. When I come to a photograph, I make sense of it just as it makes sense of me. You encounter the same photograph and *you* make your sense of it just as it makes sense of *you*. All these respective senses play in and through and with each other, intersecting across different conceptual, cultural, historical, and affective networks. But just as an oyster can send one man to the hospital, one to the bathroom, and a third to heaven, a painting, a photograph, a film affects us differently — and palpably.

Of course, most things we perceive we don't really read. We plug them directly into the familiar, the known. Want to hide from someone? Stand right in front of them. Want to be invisible? Appear just like everybody else. Isn't this the criminal's code — act normal, like you belong here? Often, we don't see what we see.

To read an image, on the other hand, is to encounter the becoming of the world. It is to be transformed. To stand before Van Gogh's sunflowers is to risk being turned to that vibrant viscosity. An image repositions us. This repositioning can be as banal and profound as shifting our perspective. For instance, look at the portrait of Lucian Freud's mother. You're standing on your two feet but, somehow, your view is peering down upon her. This is all to say that when we see an image, we don't just see the world: we see a seeing of the world.

Look at Andreas Gursky's photographs. How is it precisely these images see? This is not a vantage point anyone could enjoy. And I'm not just referring to the spatial perspective, a perspective that is strange enough, an impossible perspective, a perspective that could only come from somewhere else — from a UFO, perhaps. I'm referring to how these images see, how they gather up the world. What kind of seeing is this?

Everything is in equal focus. There is no center, no place that is distinguished from any other place. There is no hierarchy. Which is to say, there are no categories, there is no *knowing*, not even a concept. Nothing is an example of anything else such as, say, a concert or mountain or swimming pool. Gursky's images are stupid. The human and the natural are splayed along a common plane, as if these eyes — or at least this seeing — could not distinguish between human flesh and a rock. When this seeing takes up a concert or a mountain or a soccer field or a swimming pool, it can't distinguish between people, trees, lines in the terrain. Everything that enters the visual is just another mark, an inflection of space, a modulation of light. Even a shelf of Prada shoes is stripped of its cultural or iconic or referential currency. When the title utters "Prada," it's not a declaration or deadpan commentary but an almost child-like babble: Prada.

These images do not come from human eyes, from eyes enmeshed in the world. There are no referents; these are not records or monuments (even if the images are monumental). They are not expressive of anything; they do not proffer commentary on the contemporary or the dehumanization of life. Nothing has been captured; no experience has been recorded. These images are so thoroughly stupid that the human, like all other categories, never coheres, never assumes categorical distinction. No, these are not human eyes that see.

Nor are they divine. After all, God is omniscient; He certainly knows the difference between a human and a rock. It's not even the view from Olympus for while Zeus may not be omniscient, he certainly dabbles in human affairs enough to know what's what. This seeing comes from an impossible place; these eyes are neither human nor divine. They are alien eyes.

This is not an extension of our eyes but a fundamentally different way of viewing. This is an invitation to the strange. This is what makes Gursky's photographs so foreboding: when we look at them, we are not witnessing an extension of our own eyes. Nor are we looking at anything per se; these images do not proffer objects. When we look at a Gursky photograph we are not seeing things but seeing seeing, a kind of looking that is non-human and non-divine. Or rather, we see a seeing and hence see as this seeing does. To view Gursky's images is to see as an alien; to view Gursky's images is to become (with) alien.

Gursky's images are not really photographs in that they are not images taken by someone, somewhere. Gursky does not capture what he sees. On the other hand, maybe these are the *only* photographs in that they see as the camera sees — indifferently, stupidly, everything in focus. Gursky offers us camera-vision, utterly indifferent, without categorical distinctions other than the modulation of the visible. Gursky rids his art of the human, takes himself out of the picture, as it were, and lets the camera do the seeing, photographs without photography, without a photographer. This is why his images share such an affiliation with surveillance photos, photos without a photographer, without consideration, an anonymous visual sweep. (One may object that these images have been created — modified — by computer software and that, therefore, they are not camera-views. But that is to assume that the camera begins and ends with the lens. Photoshop does not come after the image; it is the camera still working.) As one views Gursky's images, then, one sees as a camera; one becomes a camera. Technology is no longer an extension of the body; the body becomes an extension of the technology.

Is alien-vision the same as camera-vision? Clearly not: while the camera is stupid, the alien may enjoy a different kind of thinking, an unrecognizable thinking, an organization of time and space and knowledge that eludes our perception, like the "certain Chinese encyclopedia" that Borges stumbles on (Foucault, OT xv). That is, whereas the camera doesn't categorize at all, the alien enjoys impossible categorizations. And yet the alien and the camera share a non-human mode of seeing. To see as a camera sees, just as to see as an alien sees, is no longer to see as a human: it is to become something else.

To read images immanently is to not reduce them to examples, derivations, symbols, or referents. It is to read them affirmatively, as modes of going in the world that include those things *in* the image as well as those invisible elements that are of the image — the affect, yes, but also the very act of seeing. It is to read an image as a conspiracy of a sort. Or, better, as a little engine, a contraption, with all sorts of moving parts that intersect other moving parts. And what does this engine make? You tell me.

Example 4. The Horror of the Image: On **The Ring**

Cujo's a dog. The blob's a blob. Freddy is a dream of revenge. What is the ring? The answer is strange: it's the image. The source of terror, fear, and death is the image. *The Ring* is an odd and surprising film.

Why, after having viewed the tape, does the phone ring? Because the phone call is an image. The phone rips the voice from the body, leaving a spectral trace, an imitation of the person on the other end: an image. When the phone rings in *The Ring*, then, it is not exterior to the visual image but is the image still happening. The voice through the receiver and the visuals on the screen are part of the same image. The ring of the phone is a metonymy of the visual image.

The Ring proffers the great paranoia of the image. It looks like us, it talks like us, it seems to have emotions. Which is to say, the image has a life of its own — but without a body. It doesn't sleep, it doesn't eat, it can't converse. In what is perhaps the creepiest scene in the movie, we see the girl-image under observation, never tiring, never shifting demeanor, never responding. Or, for that matter, becoming frenzied. This particular image may seem pissed off but under the grueling conditions of interrogation it doesn't get more pissed off. The image is not reasonable and therefore is not unreasonable. An image, it just keeps repeating itself, yielding more images, as if from nowhere, from the play of light and dark that it is.

I can see why a parent might think such a child unruly. How can one discipline an image when it won't listen to reason, when it just keeps on repeating itself? Cut off its supply of light, send it somewhere its sound can't be heard: drop it down a deep well and cover that well up. Think of the posters for the movie — a ring of darkness, light barely making its way through. This is the horror, light emerging from darkness: the birth of the image.

This girl-image was not born of woman. But then where did it come from? It wasn't recorded; it is not a memory or record but is itself a living force. No, it was not recorded: it was always already born, the image of the family, of mommy-daddy-baby. In this nightmare, this paranoia, this cliché-image has only one directive: not *watch* me, not *disseminate* me, but copy me, *copy* me over and over and over again without changing a thing.

But the image is not so easily bent to the cliché needs of the bourgeois family, the triangulation of mommy-daddy-baby. Look at the video in the film: it is avant-garde cinema. It moves across various planes, horizontal and vertical. There is no triangle here; Oedipus has exploded (pace Marc Lafia). There is no story, no transparent metaphors. In fact, these images are dense, opaque, heavy with shadow and their insistent refusal to slip into a palatable narrative.

The film hence presents two fears, two kinds of horror, in the double genitive: it is both the horror we experience of the image and the image's horror of experiencing us. There is our fear of the image, of its refusal to bend to story. So lifelike yet utterly devoid of human life, the image makes a most horrific servant and an even more horrific master. And then there is the image's fear of the narrative, of the cliché that would break it, that would make it bend to clear geometric shapes when all its wants to do is go as it goes, a decentered affective resonance. Perhaps that's why it is so angry.

20

Reading (in) the Network

The network — emails, text messages, websites, chatrooms, tweets, comments, postings, blogs — is a grand, complex metabolic engine that takes up the world and makes odd sense of it. And we, nodes in the network, read it just as it reads us, a sense-making that is at once determined and determining. We *are* the network just as we are thoroughly enmeshed in its winding tendrils.

The network is a fluid space of endless becoming that emerges at every moment — with every click, jot, note, blogpost, tweet. And even without those avatars, algorithms pour over this pixel text, rewriting it in the endless electric hum of the computational. This is a read-write engine, being written to and written over, again and again and again. The web is not just an archive. There is no real *before* that we access *now*. The web is always and already changing, morphing, the past churning in the same time as the now. The network is post-history. Or always-history, depending on how you look at it.

A book is inherently linear. Language may distend and fold the book's linearity into complex shapes and possibilities. And yet there is always a back there — flip to page three — and an up there, at page 186. In the network, there is no linearity. Or, rather, linearity is one possible configuration. The book is the recorder of a history that moves from past to present. The network is the always-writing of a history that is allatonce and always in the making.

Now, perhaps all texts are networks. As I read a book I make sense of it, just as it makes sense of me: the event of reading is a mutual becoming, a read-write event. And the book is inevitably entwined in a network of other texts — books I've read, books others have read, book reviews, courses, adaptations, citations, rhythmic influences. And we can, in some sense, say that my reading of a book writes over that book.

But the internet accelerates this network effect exponentially. Unlike the page, the computer is an active consumer of its own content, distributing and ordering content according to ever-shifting rules. And, unlike the page, internet content can be written over in real-time — and, in nearly the same breath, published. It is as voracious as it is generous.

To read this network is to write this network. You tweet; I retweet; I blog about your tweet; I email your comment on my blog about your tweet to my friend who, in turn, tweets about your tweet which you, in turn, retweet. This is a productive collision, a collusion, a distributed authorship. This is the death of the author performed every day, in multiple ways, by every Jane, Dick, and Harry.

The network text is not prescriptive. It proffers a set of tools for authoring, archiving, and playback. There are hence a variety of operations, diverse ways of reading and being read, even at the same time. Within this vast network are multiple modes of making sense of this network. This text includes — supersedes — its critiques and organizations. All action in the network is simul-taneously constituent and constitutive of the network.

Take a site — and that is already a bit of a misnomer as a site is often many sites and is actually more of a node; perhaps that is what we should call them, not websites but webnodes — such as Facebook or Stumbleupon. They are at once a personal archiving tool; a singular directory; and a recommendation engine. They make sense of the internet while being part of the internet, while literally constituting the internet.

This relentlessly involuted time makes for swift operations. The network text is fast. This is not the indulgent time-space of the book; nor is it even the lingering of an image. This speed privileges information over affect. Have you ever tried to be funny in a text? It's difficult. Language in the network becomes a kind of Morse code, signaling information, pointing the way, conveying data. It is rarely beautiful or, in and of itself, complex. This is not a criticism; this is a fact. The slick surface of the network — it is a surface architecture, an origami — does not allow for irony, for a play with depths and heights. And while it seems a perfect vehicle for dissimulation — and it is, as the rate of spam only accelerates — it is also disinclined to dissimulation. Look at Facebook: the network yields an odd kind of honesty as people pour themselves out into the network. Now look at Borges or Nabokov's *Pale Fire* and their delirious narrators. The web is itself delirious but the individual nodes tend to be peculiarly staid.

Old concepts still define our social-network behavior. We want to know where our interlocutors live, how old they are, their gender, education, their likes and dislikes. We cling to the horse and buggy even as the railway pounds by (pace McLuhan). The advent of a site and experience such as Chatroullete.com begins to introduce new architectures of the social encounter, encounters no longer tethered by the familiar anchors of place, class, clique, place in the sexual hierarchy, or financial transaction. This is the network moving so fast that is has sloughed its old skin, leaving us exposed and naked with our desires: What do you want from others?

Of course, as technology changes, so does the speed and rhythm of network reading. As pipes get fatter, media becomes more robust and perhaps slower. Take the podcast or streaming full-length films. Suddenly, amidst the hustle and bustle of the internet economy, we find these respites, this savoring, these elongated moments. Meanwhile, elsewhere on the network, encounters accelerate.

Indeed, the network remains essentially fast as every move made constitutes it. Reading the network, then, demands ever-shifting tactics of parrying, archiving, and rewriting from within the vortex. It demands all the tactics of reading anything — a book, a film, a person's face — but faster and often all at once.

Perhaps, in an odd way, reading within the network is akin to reading within the social. Just as glances and words shift while at a party — and just as your reactions and gestures shape the glances and gestures — the network is an endless stream of swift gestures that forge gestures that, in turn, shape the very network itself.

21

Teaching Immanent Reading

How does one go about teaching immanent reading? There's no right answer and yet there are good and bad readings. This of course always drives students crazy. If there's no right answer, why don't they all get As? What distinguishes one reading from another, one paper from another? And what they heck are they supposed to do, anyway?

Unfortunately, students are taught that to read a book involves learning some secret — especially "literature" and, even more, art and film which either "mean" nothing or else definitely take a very special and rare decoder ring. These students are told to map the themes and motifs and figure out what the text is really about — politics or love or technology or man vs. nature. Or else they point out all the evidence that shows that this film is, in fact, an example of New Wave cinema or the Oedipal complex or patriarchy. So when I ask them to put all this aside, all their decoder rings and readymade measuring sticks, they get a bit uncomfortable and, at times, angry.

Well, why don't they all get As? Because not all of them actually proffer good readings. Once they throw away their usual tools — character identification, cultural critique, themes — they tend to end up listing aspects of the book or film or piece of art. And often they notice some interesting things such as a shift in voice from an "I" to a "we." But they don't know what to do with this piece of evidence. "So what?" I often scribble in the margins of their papers. "What happens when the voice shifts from first-person singular to first-person plural?"

They usually then think that I'm contradicting myself: "You told us not to say what the text means. So I just wrote what I noticed."

"Yes," I reply, "but you still haven't told me *how* this work performs, what it does, *how* it works the reader over, what kinds of affects and effects it proffers. And, most importantly, you haven't brought this text to life. You have not made me see it in a new light. You pointed something out I may have missed but you haven't told me why I should care about it."

A good reading brings the thing to life and makes the world see it as if for the very first time, just as Gabriel Kolko does with the USDA, Carroll Smith-Rosenberg with the Victorian woman, Nietzsche with Christianity, Foucault with sexuality. All of these readings take the evidence, the diverse components of a text, and rearrange them so that we see those things again, anew, fresh. They don't just point out inconsistencies or oddities; they arrange the evidence just so, into a shape that is coherent and enjoys its own logic.

So what does happen when the text moves form "I" to "we"? Well, it moves from the singular to the collective and includes the reader; it moves from a certain distance to a certain inclusiveness. So what? What happens when the text does this? Is it trying to make me, the reader, complicit? Do I now feel complicit? To what effect? To what affect? In other words, what is this text *doing* — to me, to the world, to itself — when it shifts voice? And how does this action relate to *what* the text is saying?

Teaching students to read this way is not easy. After all, I can't simply map the themes and symbols on the board and have the students memorize them. This is not biology. I can't just tell them which veins lead where. In fact, there is nothing per se to teach. I teach skills.

How does one teach students to read well? There is nothing to memorize, no checklist to employ. All I can do is show them what a good reading is. All I can do is offer example after example. Example, you say? I thought this was not exemplary reading. Well, it's not. I do not offer examples of a concept or genre or idea. I offer examples that are examples of themselves — or what

I call *pure exemplarity*. Each reading performs a different reading; each is an example of difference. This is not a hierarchical example but one of an infinite series of examples that reveal that each thing goes as it goes.

I want each student to read the text in his or her own way and I want each to do it engagingly, interestingly, thoroughly. So one thing I do is give them lots and lots of readings so they know what a reading looks like. It's much like a fielding coach teaching a shortstop to field ground balls. He can't just tell him what to do; he has actually to hit groundball after groundball until the fielder gets a *sense* for how the ball can go, the sudden jumps it can make, the rolls it can take. That is what I do in the classroom: we perform reading after reading until the students begin to get a sense for how texts can do, the types of moves they can make. My students don't learn this or that — facts, figures, theories; they learn how to approach things and make sense of them.

One thing I always tell my students, one approach that is almost always surprising and illuminative, is to focus on the relationship between what a text says and how it says it. Most (non)readers just look at what a text says. By including *how* it says it, and how this *how* inflects the *what* and vice-versa, a reading necessarily brings something forth that may not have been obvious. But this does not mean to look for contradiction; this is not a call to witch-hunt hypocrites. The what and the how are in a relationship of mutual inflection, not necessarily contradiction. Socrates, for example, seemingly contradicts himself but it is not a contradiction: it's irony, the two claims — the how and the what — effacing and propelling each other in a relentless feedback loop. And it is precisely that relationship that is Socrates' argument.

Another approach is to highlight some seemingly irrelevant detail — someone's name, a sub-title, a theme song, the opening credits — and argue how it inflects and performs the text as a whole, undoing it, condensing it, qualifying it, complicating it.

This is still kind of obtuse. Here, then, is what I hope is a more practical approach to learning how to perform an immanent reading.

Assemble the data. Write down everything you notice that seems to stand out. For instance, if it's a book:

a. What explicit argument or arguments does it make? John Austin refers to this as the constative claims of an utterance or text.

b. How is the book structured? *The Canterbury Tales* are structured quite differently than, say, *War and Peace*. Or take Nietzsche, for whom form is an explicit argument, his non-systematic approach a critique of systematic philosophy.

c. What is the rhythm of the prose? Do the sentences stretch and wind, as in Pynchon's *Gravity's Rainbow*? Are they curt, incisive, as in Palahniuk's *Fight Club*?

d. In what voice is the book written? This includes the grammatical person — first, second, third — as well its tone. Consider *Pale Fire*, for example, and its famously unreliable narrator.

e. Are there recurring figures? Nietzsche returns to smell, the body, blood, digestion; Burroughs to control, aliens, viruses, semen. A good reading accounts for how these figures figure.

What physical traits does this thing have? Is it light? Heavy? Short? Long? This probably refers more to an object than a book but it might still matter with a book. Marshall McLuhan's *The Medium is the Massage* is printed small, pocket-size, as if it were a portable manual or map to the electronic age.

a. What affective traits does it have? What is the mood of this thing? Is it somber and morose? Serious and strident? Is it playful, funny, strange? Write these down.

b. What is its posture? That is, how does it stand towards the world? How does it stand towards the reader? Nietzsche, for instance, alienates himself from both the world and the viewer — and yet he does write and so he must seek some kind of reaction from his readers. If it's an object, how is it oriented? How does it stand? Is it firmly rooted in the ground? Does it sway with the wind? Is it seeable all at once? A tree goes differently than a tulip, a blade of grass, a field of grass, a vine.

c. What else? Does it have a title? A sub-title? What does it remind you of? Why? That is, follow it to see if it might forge connections with other things.

And now comes the hard part: putting it all together. This is the part that takes skill, an ability to assemble, make connections, stitch different things together while allowing them to be strange, different, to be themselves. A good reader not only embraces but seeks and amplifies the ambivalences, multivalences, ambiguities, and complexity of a text. Let the world be strange.

How does one teach this? How does one teach the way of things? We teach observation, yes, but how do we teach assemblage? It is at once quite practical (do it over and over, with different texts, different things) and absolutely mysterious (why one person can make such and such connections and another cannot belies science). Such is the way of art. Such is the way of reckoning a moving world while moving oneself. There are no rules other than heed difference and don't reduce, amplify; no principles other than be generous, perhaps thorough, but always generous. When it comes to teaching the different ways things can relate to each other, when it comes to forging the very terms of sense, well, this is an elusive art.

You might try what's called a mind map. You write everything down on one page — all the things you notice, all the physical and affective traits, all the data. With it splayed before you, you start making connections. Does the sub-title relate to something you notice in the text? For instance, the sub-title of Nietzsche' *Ecce Homo* is "How One Becomes What One Is." You also have written down that *Ecce Homo* is written in sections that don't add up to any one point: the text itself is a becoming. *Ah-ha!* Draw a line between them. Use circles, squares, triangles; use arrows, lines, dotted or otherwise. Group related items together. See if the groups relate to each other. See what's extraneous.

I often teach using what I call an argument map. A critical essay about anything — a reading — should have anywhere from three to five key turns, moments that define the shape of the argument, voluptuous or sharp turns of thinking. The goal of the argument map is to force the reader/writer to articulate these key points *and then explain the connection between the points*. This is the thing that is hard to teach: the manner in which different things relate to each other. This is why I forbid the use of words and phrases such as "also," "furthermore," and "in addition." These words are not turns of argument, of thinking, of assemblage; they are terms of listing. Words of thinking include "but," "however," "then," "on the contrary," "therefore," "that is to say." Each of these moves thinking elsewhere — "but," "however," "on the contrary" mark turns, changes of direction; "then" and "therefore" mark link lines of thought.

As with every art, practice is essential. The more one reads, the more one reads readings, the better one gets.

22

A Note on Rhetoric, with Reference
to Foucault

The dictum of the sophists is strange and beautiful: Say the right thing at the right time. What's so odd is that it at once proffers an absolute (the right thing) and a locality (at the right time). While rhetoric is often accused of being without standards, the opposite is true: it has as many standards as there are circumstances. For the rhetor, it's not that there is no propriety, it's that propriety can never be known for sure beforehand. Propriety emerges — here, there, and everywhere, all the time.

Whenever a rhetor is asked about what's right, his response is usually the same: *it depends*. Circumstance is local and so is propriety. And, to make things even stranger, there is no propriety to a circumstance per se as a circumstance is itself a network of events and perspectives. And each perspective is itself a network of trajectories of history, memory, desire, need. Nothing is more mysterious and difficult than doing the right thing at the right time.

How does one teach such a sense of propriety? If you look at the rhetorics through history, the *technes* — rhetoric is a *techne*, a way of doing — they are filled with examples. In such-and-such a situation, so-and-so said this; in this other situation, so-and-so said this. The sophist is the fielding coach, hitting ball after ball to his students until the student/fielders understand the way of argument, of circumstance, of perspective.

In *The Use of Pleasure*, Foucault discovers the art of reading the body immanently. He discovers a rhetoric of appetite. The Greeks, Foucault tells us, did not discipline their bodies according to external criteria. Rather, they heeded an odd sort of principle, *chresis aprhodision*, the use of pleasure. It is an odd principle for it is not determinative per se; it is not a fixed guideline nor a set of "universal and uniform rules" (106): "Regimen should not be understood as a corpus of universal and uniform rules; it was more in the nature of a manual for reacting to situations in which one might find oneself, a treatise for adjusting one's behavior to fit the circumstances" (106). The propriety of the situation is circumstantial, determined by that situation. It is, as Foucault discovers, "[a] question of right use," of doing the right or appropriate thing. And yet this propriety is not to be fixed: "It was much more a question of a variable adjustment in which one had to take different factors into account" (53).

It's not that there is no propriety for the sophist. On the contrary, propriety is something that needs to be heeded *all the time*. And so a propriety, yes, but a propriety that moves, that changes. A "good" regimen is one that is adaptable, that opens up possibilities rather than limiting them: "A regimen was not good if it only permitted one to live in one place, with one type of food, and if it did not allow one to be open to any change. The usefulness of a regimen lay precisely in the possibility it gave individuals to face different situations" (105). A regimen is not fixed in time; on the contrary, it's temporal. Indeed, the three main factors to be considered in the body's regulations were need, social status, and *timeliness* (53–54). This rhetoric of pleasure is not a matter of fixed spaces, of finding and deter- mining the right geometric coordinates. As time enters the equation, the geometric planes are put in motion and the question of reading the body shifts from one of geometry to one of calculus: it is now a question of "how best to *calculate* the opportune times and appropriate frequencies" of consumption (116).

This rhetorics of the body turns on time. But not just time as an abstract generality, *but the right time*, or what rhetors call *kairos*. If a regimen could somehow rigorously account for bodily need and availability; if such a regimen could uniformly codify social conditions, what would forever elude such a regimen is *kairos*, the right time to act. Chow Yun-Fat as The Killer may know his guns and his body's limitations, but this does not tell him the right time to shoot. Michael Jordan may know the rules and plays of basketball inside and out but this knowledge does not inform him when and in what way to take the ball to the basket. A Greek nobleman may enjoy wine and young boys, but this does not tell him the best time to indulge his pleasures; he must act "at the right time and in the right amount" (57). For the Greeks, Foucault discovers, *kairos* informs not just the ethical question of pleasure but permeates all matters of "technique" as one must be "able to determine the moment when it was necessary to act and the precise manner in which to do so in terms of existing circumstances" (58).

In "the use of pleasure," Foucault discovers a structure that moves and changes according to the spatio-temporal configuration of all the participants, a protean standard, as Lohren Green writes. There are rules of a sort, but the rules do not regulate and determine from afar but are determined from *within* the situation. Reading the body is not a matter of looking elsewhere, of looking to external codes. On the contrary, reading the body involves a rigorous individualizing:

> [H]ere everything was a matter of adjustment, circumstance, and personal position... Therefore, in this form of morality, the individual did not make himself into an ethical subject by universalizing the principles that informed his action; on the contrary, he did so by means of an attitude and a quest that individualized his action, modulated it. (62)

The appropriate is not a generality. Rather, it emerges from a particular circumstance as a particularity. Propriety is configured by and through difference, by and through this or that.

Picture two parents of two different children. One says to his 16 year old, "No drinking tonight!" The other says, "Be safe. Do the right thing." This yields two very different kinds of negotiation of propriety. For the first adolescent the law is clear: no booze, no matter what. To the second, a drink may be fine; two drinks may be fine; 20 drinks may be fine. It all depends on his or her body, on what's happening. Which is to say, alcohol is not bad in and of itself. It's the event of drinking, the how and when and where and who that matters. There are good and bad ways of drinking. How do we know which is which? Well, that is elusive but we do certainly know based on an ever-shifting set of criteria. And, most of the time, an event such as drinking alcohol is not good or bad; there's some good, there's some bad, there's some indifference, there's some interesting, some banality.

The logic and practice of heeding this very strange, protean propriety has a name, an ancient name: rhetoric. Perhaps, then, we can call our immanent reading by this more familiar name. We can call it rhetoric.

23

Why Immanent Reading?

To read immanently means to stand towards things — towards the world, towards oneself — with a different posture: with poise and curiosity, with generosity and a will to multiplicity. It is to ask different questions: not "what does this mean?" but "what does this do?" Not "how does this fit into what I know?" but "how does this create new ways of knowing?"

To read a text immanently is not a matter of discovering what school or movement it inhabits but what school or movement the text *inaugurates*. I once taught a graduate seminar at an art school. For the final assignment, students had to invent an art movement, tracing its history, proffering its position. Reading like this is not matter of fixing a thing in place but of propelling it into new territory, discovering its networks, how its tendrils reach across time, place, discipline. Deleuze discovers Bacon's image in the haptic territory of the Egyptians, moving between eyes and hands (Deleuze, FB 10). William Burroughs does not break the laws of literature as if the laws pre-existed; he *invents* the laws, an entire grammar of undulation, a most surprising ethics.

And as we engage things, they engage back and ask: What will we become?

By abandoning signifiers and symbols as the sole mode of sense-making, we are not abandoning concepts, sense, and language. We are introducing new modes of making sense of things, new technologies of reading.

To read the way of things is to participate in the great becoming of the cosmos. But it does not happen automatically. It is a matter of paying keen attention to what's happening while happening oneself, a collide-o-scopic encounter that sees more than just the presumed significant.

Look at Georges Perec, sitting in a café, drinking a beer and having a look around:

> Note down what you can see. Anything worthy of note going on. Do you know how to see what's worthy of note? Is there anything that strikes you?
>
> Nothing strikes you. You don't know how to see.
>
> You must set about it more slowly, almost stupidly. Force yourself to write down what is of no interest, what is most obvious, most common, most colourless. (50)

To Perec, one can only be intimate when one is rid of the familiar, when one allows the strange to speak, when one throws away the ready-mades and reaches for the world with a certain poise, with a surge that awaits and creates in the same gesture.

There is a friction in this engagement with things, a heat that comes from closely following the contours of this or that. The chiasm sizzles. It is a friction born of the question: How does this go? Where can I take it? Where can it take me? It is the friction of becoming and it is delirious.

And it is here, in this heat and teem, that life happens, that life flourishes, that Yes and its great health reside. It is here we find not just joy and not just ethics — the ethics of generosity — but the joy of an ethics, the joy of generosity. It is here that the health of the reader and the health of the world coincide, even when mutually indifferent.

Our goal is to become with the way of things. And in so doing to become more intimate with the world, more intimate with ourselves. This is our pleasure, this is our demand, this is our delight: to become with the world.

Works Cited

Austin, J.L., *How to Do Things with Words*, Second Edition (Cambridge, MA: Harvard UP, 1962, 1975).

Barthes, Roland, "The Death of the Author," in *Image, Music, Text*, tr. Heath (New York: Noonday Press, 1977).

Bergson, Henri, *Matter and Memory*, tr. Paul and Palmer (New York: Zone Books, 1988).

Burroughs, William S., *My Education* (New York: Viking, 1995).

—, *Place of Dead Roads* (New York: Picador, 1983).

—, *Naked Lunch* (New York: Grove, 1959): "Junk yields a basic formula of 'evil' virus: *The Algebra of Need*. The face of 'evil' is always the face of total need."

—, "The Discipline of DE," in *Exterminator!* (New York: Penguin, 1966).

—, *The Cat Inside* (New York: Viking, 1986): "Elegance, grace, delicacy, beauty, and a lack of self-consciousness: a creature who knows he is cute soon isn't."

—, *The Western Lands* (New York: Penguin 1987).

Canguilhem, Georges, *The Normal and the Pathological* (New York: Zone Books, 1978).

de Certeau, Michel, *The Practice of Everyday Life*, tr. Rendall (Berkeley: UC Berkeley P, 1984).

Deleuze, Gilles, *Cinema 1: The Movement-Image*, tr. Tomlinson and Habberjam (Minneapolis: U of Minnesota P, 1986).

—, *Cinema 2: The Time-Image*, tr. Galeta and Tomlinson (Minneapolis: U of Minnesota P, 1989).

—, *Difference and Repetition*, tr. Patton (New York: Columbia UP, 1994).

—, *The Fold: Leibniz and the Baroque*, tr. Conley (Minneapolis: U of Minnesota P, 1993).

—, *Francis Bacon: The Logic of Sensation*, tr. Smith (Minneapolis: U of Minnesota P, 2003).

Deleuze, Gilles and Félix Guattari, *A Thousand Plateaus*, tr. Massumi (Minneapolis: U of Minnesota P, 1987).

Deleuze, Gilles and Claire Parnet, *Dialogues II*, tr. Tomlinson and Habberjam, (New York: Columbia UP, 1977).

Derrida, Jacques, *Of Grammatology*, tr. Spivak (Baltimore: Johns Hopkins UP, 1974).

Foucault, Michel, *The History of Sex, v1*, tr. Hurley (New York: Vintage, 1978).

—, *The Order of Things* (New York: Vintage Books, 1973).

—, *The Use of Pleasure*, tr. Hurley (New York: Vintage, 1990).

Gadamer, Hans-Georg, *Truth and Method*, tr. Weisenheimer and Marshall (New York: Crossroad, 1990).

Green, Lohren, *Poetical Dictionary*, (Berkeley: Atelos, 2003).

Gysin, Brion, *The Process*, (London: Quartet Books, 1969).

Kant, Immanuel, *The Critique of Judgment*, tr. Pluhar (Indianapolis: Hackett Publishing Co., 1987).

McLuhan, Marshall and Quentin Fiore, *Medium is the Massage*, (Corte Madera: Gingko Press, 1996).

Merleau-Ponty, Maurice, "The Chiasm," in *The Visible and the Invisible*, tr. Lingis (Evanston: Northwestern UP, 1968).

—, *The Phenomenology of Perception*, tr. Smith (London and New York: Routledge, 1962).

—, *The Prose of the World*, tr. O'Neill (Evanston: Northwestern UP, 1973).

—, *Sense and Non-Sense*, tr. Dreyfus and Dreyfus (Evanston: Northwestern UP, 1964).

—, *Signs*, tr. Richard C. McCleary (Evanston: Northwestern UP, 1964).

Nietzsche, Friedrich, *On the Genealogy of Morals and Ecce Homo*, tr. Kaufmann and Hollingdale (New York: Vintage, 1967).

—, *On Rhetoric and Language*, eds. Gilman, Blair, and Parent (Oxford: Oxford UP, 1989).

Perec, Georges, *Species of Spaces and Other Pieces* (New York: Penguin, 2008).

Ricoeur, Paul, *Hermeneutics and the Human Sciences*, tr. Thompson (Paris: Cambridge UP, 1981).

Robertson, Lisa, *Nilling*, (Canada: Bookthug, 2012).

Contemporary culture has eliminated both the concept of the public and the figure of the intellectual. Former public spaces – both physical and cultural – are now either derelict or colonized by advertising. A cretinous anti-intellectualism presides, cheerled by expensively educated hacks in the pay of multinational corporations who reassure their bored readers that there is no need to rouse themselves from their interpassive stupor. The informal censorship internalized and propagated by the cultural workers of late capitalism generates a banal conformity that the propaganda chiefs of Stalinism could only ever have dreamt of imposing. Zer0 Books knows that another kind of discourse – intellectual without being academic, popular without being populist – is not only possible: it is already flourishing, in the regions beyond the striplit malls of so-called mass media and the neurotically bureaucratic halls of the academy. Zer0 is committed to the idea of publishing as a making public of the intellectual. It is convinced that in the unthinking, blandly consensual culture in which we live, critical and engaged theoretical reflection is more important than ever before.

ZERO BOOKS

If this book has helped you to clarify an idea, solve a problem or extend your knowledge, you may like to read more titles from Zero Books. Recent bestsellers are:

Capitalist Realism Is there no alternative?
Mark Fisher
An analysis of the ways in which capitalism has presented itself as the only realistic political-economic system.
Paperback: November 27, 2009 978-1-84694-317-1 $14.95 £7.99.
eBook: July 1, 2012 978-1-78099-734-6 $9.99 £6.99.

The Wandering Who? A study of Jewish identity politics
Gilad Atzmon
An explosive unique crucial book tackling the issues of Jewish Identity Politics and ideology and their global influence.
Paperback: September 30, 2011 978-1-84694-875-6 $14.95 £8.99.
eBook: September 30, 2011 978-1-84694-876-3 $9.99 £6.99.

Clampdown Pop-cultural wars on class and gender
Rhian E. Jones
Class and gender in Britpop and after, and why 'chav' is a feminist issue.
Paperback: March 29, 2013 978-1-78099-708-7 $14.95 £9.99.
eBook: March 29, 2013 978-1-78099-707-0 $7.99 £4.99.

The Quadruple Object
Graham Harman
Uses a pack of playing cards to present Harman's metaphysical system of fourfold objects, including human access, Heidegger's indirect causation, panpsychism and ontography.
Paperback: July 29, 2011 978-1-84694-700-1 $16.95 £9.99.

Weird Realism Lovecraft and Philosophy
Graham Harman
As Hölderlin was to Martin Heidegger and Mallarmé to Jacques
Derrida, so is H.P. Lovecraft to the Speculative Realist philoso-
phers.
Paperback: September 28, 2012 978-1-78099-252-5 $24.95 £14.99.
eBook: September 28, 2012 978-1-78099-907-4 $9.99 £6.99.

Sweetening the Pill or How We Got Hooked on Hormonal Birth
Control
Holly Grigg-Spall
Is it really true? Has contraception liberated or oppressed women?
Paperback: September 27, 2013 978-1-78099-607-3 $22.95 £12.99.
eBook: September 27, 2013 978-1-78099-608-0 $9.99 £6.99.

Why Are We The Good Guys? Reclaiming Your Mind From The
Delusions Of Propaganda
David Cromwell
A provocative challenge to the standard ideology that Western
power is a benevolent force in the world.
Paperback: September 28, 2012 978-1-78099-365-2 $26.95 £15.99.
eBook: September 28, 2012 978-1-78099-366-9 $9.99 £6.99.

The Truth about Art Reclaiming quality
Patrick Doorly
The book traces the multiple meanings of art to their various
sources, and equips the reader to choose between them.
Paperback: August 30, 2013 978-1-78099-841-1 $32.95 £19.99.

Bells and Whistles More Speculative Realism
Graham Harman
In this diverse collection of sixteen essays, lectures, and interviews
Graham Harman lucidly explains the principles of Speculative
Realism, including his own object-oriented philosophy.

Paperback: November 29, 2013 978-1-78279-038-9 $26.95 £15.99.
eBook: November 29, 2013 978-1-78279-037-2 $9.99 £6.99.

Towards Speculative Realism: Essays and Lectures Essays and
Lectures
Graham Harman
These writings chart Harman's rise from Chicago sportswriter to
co founder of one of Europe's most promising philosophical
movements: Speculative Realism.
Paperback: November 26, 2010 978-1-84694-394-2 $16.95 £9.99.
eBook: January 1, 1970 978-1-84694-603-5 $9.99 £6.99.

Meat Market Female flesh under capitalism
Laurie Penny
A feminist dissection of women's bodies as the fleshy fulcrum of
capitalist cannibalism, whereby women are both consumers and
consumed.
Paperback: April 29, 2011 978-1-84694-521-2 $12.95 £6.99.
eBook: May 21, 2012 978-1-84694-782-7 $9.99 £6.99.

Translating Anarchy The Anarchism of Occupy Wall Street
Mark Bray
An insider's account of the anarchists who ignited Occupy Wall
Street.
Paperback: September 27, 2013 978-1-78279-126-3 $26.95 £15.99.
eBook: September 27, 2013 978-1-78279-125-6 $6.99 £4.99.

One Dimensional Woman
Nina Power
Exposes the dark heart of contemporary cultural life by
examining pornography, consumer capitalism and the ideology of
women's work.
Paperback: November 27, 2009 978-1-84694-241-9 $14.95 £7.99.
eBook: July 1, 2012 978-1-78099-737-7 $9.99 £6.99.

Dead Man Working

Carl Cederstrom, Peter Fleming

An analysis of the dead man working and the way in which capital is now colonizing life itself.

Paperback: May 25, 2012 978-1-78099-156-6 $14.95 £9.99.

eBook: June 27, 2012 978-1-78099-157-3 $9.99 £6.99.

Unpatriotic History of the Second World War

James Heartfield

The Second World War was not the Good War of legend. James Heartfield explains that both Allies and Axis powers fought for the same goals - territory, markets and natural resources.

Paperback: September 28, 2012 978-1-78099-378-2 $42.95 £23.99.

eBook: September 28, 2012 978-1-78099-379-9 $9.99 £6.99.

Find more titles at www.zero-books.net